The Angels'
Game

The Angels' Game

A HANDBOOK OF MODERN DIPLOMACY

William Macomber

𝕤𝕕

STEIN AND DAY/*Publishers*/New York

First published in 1975
Copyright © 1975 by William B. Macomber
All rights reserved
Designed by David Miller
Printed in the United States of America
Stein and Day/*Publishers*/Scarborough House,
Briarcliff Manor, N.Y. 10510

The author has assigned the proceeds from
this book to the American Foreign Service
Scholarship Fund.

Library of Congress Cataloging in Publication Data

Macomber, William B   1921–
    The angels' game.

    Bibliography: p.
    Includes index.
    1.   Diplomacy.   I.   Title.
JX1662.M27   327'.2   74-29319
ISBN 0-8128-1791-5

To Phyllis
My chère collègue

PREFACE

DIPLOMATS AND THE ORGANIZATIONS for which they work, whether called state departments or foreign offices, tend to have a far better understanding of what their job used to be than of what it is today. This is hardly surprising in view of the rapid and far-reaching changes that have taken place in diplomacy since World War II. Given the world we live in, the same can be said of most human institutions and activities.

This book is about the requirements of today's diplomacy. It has been written in the hope that readers, in and out of the profession, will find it helpful in gaining a fuller understanding of what, under much altered circumstances, the modern diplomat's job is all about.

It is impossible adequately to record how much a book of this kind owes to others. Classic writers of earlier times, and today's diplomats from many lands, have contributed far more than I can properly hope to acknowledge.

Above all, I owe a special debt to my colleagues, past and present, of the United States State Department and of the Foreign Service of the United States. These distinguished men and women have been my most patient, persistent, and effective teachers. They continue so to this day.

The pages which follow offer neither a detailed history of diplomacy nor a technical compendium of diplomatic procedures. Both are important, but both are well covered elsewhere. Rather as a guide to the modern profession, they will examine the classic qualities and skills it still requires. They will examine, too, the new qualities and skills made mandatory now by diplomacy's much altered environment and expanded dimensions.

It is a book which has been written in the midst of an active diplomatic assignment, largely in a series of brief stints in the pre-breakfast hours. The fact of its active-duty preparation should not, however, be misconstrued. It has no coloration of an official treatise, and it is, of course, a personal effort entirely.

WILLIAM MACOMBER

Ankara, Turkey

CONTENTS

The Angels'
Game

CHAPTER ONE

Diplomacy: Then and Now

LONG AGO IT WAS ASSERTED that the first diplomats were angels. Their task, it was said, was to carry messages between heaven and earth. "This is not," Sir Harold Nicolson later noted, "a view which would be held by modern historians."

In the public mind, too, the diplomatic profession has never enjoyed such a lofty association. Unfortunately, and somewhat unfairly, quite the opposite has been true.

"A diplomat is an honest man sent to lie abroad for his country," wrote Sir Henry Wooten in 1604, and his words seem indelibly inscribed in history's memory. Overlooked is the fact that far from being accepted, this statement brought an end to Sir Henry's diplomatic career. In vain did he seek to explain it as a "mere merriment." His outraged employer, James I, would never use him again. There is a second axiom also ascribed to him, more accurate but less widely known. *Animas fiere sapientiores quiescendo*, he later wrote—"in retirement we grow wiser."

For the truth is that diplomacy, if it adheres to its proper objectives and most effective methods, is an honorable profession. To the degree it remains committed to the search for peace, it can be an exalted one as well.

It can also be unusually interesting and satisfying. In 1716 François de Callières concluded his classic treatise by noting that disappointments in life await everyone. "But in no profession," he added,

13

"are disappointments so amply outweighed by such rich opportunities as in the practice of diplomacy."

It is still true. But it is true with important provisos. The modern diplomat can function only if he first comprehends and adjusts to the changed circumstances of his profession. He must then commit a lifetime to the mastery of those critical qualities and skills, old as well as new, which modern diplomacy requires. Otherwise, de Callières's rich opportunities will pass him by.

Diplomacy is not a term with an always agreed upon meaning. I have before me, for example, roughly a dozen definitions, culled from dictionaries, encyclopedias, and the writings of well-known authorities. No two are exactly the same.

Modern usage, however, generally employs the word in two basic senses. First is the policy sense, as when one speaks of approving a nation's diplomacy, meaning the foreign policies which govern its relations with other nations. The second refers to the carrying out of foreign policy: that is the actual conduct of these relations. Professional diplomats, in turn, are those officials whom their governments have employed full time in support of their diplomatic efforts. The focus of professional diplomats is on policy execution, rather than on policy formation. They have, however, an important role in both.

Diplomacy, within these contexts, has existed since nation-states began. The concept of a diplomat, or rather of a professional diplomat, is much newer. Diplomacy in its initial stage did not employ permanent personnel. Officials were recruited for a particular mission. These missions were of limited duration. When their work was done, they returned home and were disbanded.

Their initial role was not dissimilar to that of the angels already referred to; they carried messages. Thus, in the earliest, most primitive stages of diplomacy, nations sent heralds to neighboring states. Back home, however, these officials had quasi-religious duties. These were carried out under the patronage of Hermes, a popular figure in ancient mythology, but one forever associated with guile and trickery. Some would say this launched diplomacy on a course which plagues it to this day.

In any event, heralds discharged their diplomatic duties by shouting messages and returning home. They required only strong lung power and an accurate memory, the latter remaining, however, to this day an important ingredient of the profession they initiated.

Later, in a somewhat more sophisticated stage, nations sent orators to deal in persuasion rather than heralds to trumpet announcements. This, obviously, marked an advance in diplomacy, although with it came certain risks. In an age when diplomatic courtesy was hardly established, there was always the danger of a reply such as that given by the Spartans to visiting ambassadors from Samos. "We have forgotten the beginning of your harangue," they said. "We paid no heed to the middle of it, and nothing has given us pleasure in it except the end."

The Romans did not make enduring contributions to diplomatic methods. Perhaps this was so because their emissaries were usually soldiers, come as conquerors. But they did advance the concept of international law. They must be credited, too, with fostering "the habit of peace."

With the Byzantines came the concept of adding observation and reporting to the duties of the diplomat. Correctly or not, it is also the Byzantines who get credit for nurturing in diplomacy a willingness to influence by fair means or foul.

In all these stages in diplomacy's development, the concept of envoys permanently in place was virtually unknown. That practice came rather late and is credited to the Italian city-states. There in the fifteenth century the idea of continuing negotiations and permanent missions first began to flourish.

Later, the Italian pattern was copied in France, where Richelieu was an important and early supporter, and by other nations as well. At the Congress of Vienna in 1815, and in the subsequent agreements of the Congress of Aix-la-Chapelle, this new pattern of permanent diplomacy was codified. Thereafter its status, ranks, and rules were firmly established by international agreement.

The system formalized at that time established the structure in which diplomacy and full-time diplomats were to operate for years to come. It endured with remarkably little change until World War II, and it exerts an extraordinary grip on all foreign offices and career diplomats to this day.

For many years the United States' participation in this system was a limited one. The early days of the Republic produced an unusually dis inguished diplomatic effort, conducted by such notable figures and accomplished diplomats as Benjamin Franklin, John Jay, Thomas Jefferson, and John and John Quincy Adams. That effort soon deteriorated, as the focus of the United States turned inward. Protected by large oceans and small neighbors, we lost interest in events beyond our shores.

We maintained permanent missions abroad but these generally focused on consular work, that is, on protecting the interests of Americans living or traveling abroad. To the degree the United States became involved in important political negotiations, these tended to be handled by the Secretary of State in Washington and by the foreign diplomats stationed there.

With some notable exceptions, the quality of our envoys also sharply deteriorated from the high standards set at the start. This was in part the logical result of the government's interests turning inward. It was the result in large part, too, of the early arrival on the scene of the political spoils system, in a particularly virulent and persistent form.

Symbolized by Senator William Learned Marcy's famous cry of "To the victors belong the spoils," it gathered momentum in the 1830's and endured long after most modern nations had developed professional diplomatic services. Moreover, it prevailed in a nearly completely untrammeled way for decades after reform had come at home, and a domestic career civil service had been established.

It was, in fact, not until 1907 and 1924, respectively, that career consular and career diplomatic services worthy of the name were created. Because of this, and because of the earlier nature and purposes of our missions abroad, probably not until after World War I did the United States become a full-fledged participant in the international diplomatic system, carrying on what was thought of elsewhere as a normal diplomatic effort.

Perhaps the most striking thing about the system which the United States thus somewhat belatedly joined was its remarkably change-resistant character. No institution, of course, resists change altogether. But in a relative sense it changed very little, and certainly the changes which did take place were small indeed compared to those which did not.

The objectives that it sought, the range of tactics that it used, the style it developed, the type of people it employed, all remained unusually constant. This was certainly so for the period from 1815 to World War I, and it was remarkably so for the period reaching all the way back to its city-state origins in the fifteenth century.

Similarly its organizational structure followed a pattern almost everywhere accepted and rarely altered through the years. Each nation operated through a series of small permanent missions abroad. These were engaged in continuing dealings with host government officials. They were led by an ambassador, minister, or consul and operated as branch offices for their foreign offices back home.

During the latter portion of this period—that is, from the Congress of Vienna to World War II—almost the only significant development in the mechanics of diplomacy was the invention of the telegraph. This was expected to revolutionize the profession, but in the period being described, it had surprisingly little effect. The gradual arrival of the airplane, similarly, had little impact. The initial conclusions that diplomats were now to become mere puppets on a string proved false, and a tenacious system proceeded very much as before.

But change is the law of life. It governs the life of nations, and of people, and of institutions. And with the passing of World War II, change—irrestible and far-reaching—finally came to this change-resistant institution. Suddenly the diplomat found he had lost his exclusive patent on his own business. The nearly private preserve in which he had operated for centuries was gone.

As noted a moment ago, nations for hundreds of years had conducted their official business with each other almost exclusively through their foreign offices and through the embassies, legations, and consulates which operated as those foreign offices' branch offices abroad. Occasionally special emissaries outside this system were employed. With the additional exception of a relatively few attachés, military and civilian, the overseas installations were entirely manned by diplomats. At the same time their parent institutions back home conducted foreign affairs with a minimum of interference from other domestic departments of government, whose interests and responsibilities were elsewhere.

With the shrinking world and the explosion in communications of the post-World War II era, all this was suddenly changing. Other government elements were dramatically and legitimately getting directly involved. State departments and foreign offices soon found themselves only one among many government departments playing a direct role in foreign affairs. Not only did every department of the executive branch of most modern governments now have interests abroad, but most subsections of these departments as well. And an astonishing number had actual activities abroad.

The diplomat also now had to contend with large new entities such as aid, information, and intelligence agencies. These had not even existed when he entered his profession. Abroad, the diplomat suddenly found himself a minority in his "own" embassy. In the case of the United States, that minority soon became a small one. State Department personnel now hovers in the neighborhood of 15 per cent of the total personnel assigned to our embassies overseas.

Accustomed to seeing the world change, the diplomat was not at all accustomed to seeing his own role buffeted in this way. It was to become a disquieting experience; and the search for a fuller understanding of his new role, and the legitimate new role of others, has been difficult and troubling. Nor has it been aided by the actions of rival government departments. Some of these, motivated by bureaucratic competitiveness and a determination to ensure their own new place in foreign affairs, have consistently sought to reduce and demean the diplomat's role.

It has been aided even less by the reaction of many of the diplomat's own colleagues. Some have been unwilling to recognize what has happened to their profession. They have doggedly lived out their lives and careers as if they were still operating in the pre-World War II era. The need to adjust to modern circumstances simply slides by them and is ignored.

Other diplomats, fully comprehending the dimensions of change which have beset their profession, react in an equally impractical fashion. They, too, resist all constructive solutions for the present, and instead call loudly and continually for a return to the good old days when everyone stayed out of their business.

It is difficult to know which of these groups is the least helpful—those with their heads in the sand, or those whose only solution is a return to the womb.

CHAPTER TWO

Hazards of the Angels' Game

THE DEFINING OF ALTERED RESPONSIBILITIES in a changing environment has been, and from now on is likely always to remain, one of the most difficult of the problems facing the modern diplomat. But there are others, too, of a more traditional nature.

There is the continuing problem, for example, of having to operate in an atmosphere of resentment and distrust. "Unlike the military, the diplomat," Jules Combon has written, "is not the spoilt child of history." His achievements are less noted than his failures. The fact that in his profession there can be drama and courage, and even grandeur, is little understood. Instead, the image of sharp practice, secrecy, and deceit lingers to plague him. So, too, does the aroma of snobbery, cookie pushing, and striped pants. It is not a reputation calculated to win either the respect or the confidence of fellow citizens.

He must contend with other misleading caricatures as well. In the public mind he is often considered a clerk merely carrying out orders. On other occasions he will find himself cast as the principal architect of his nation's foreign policy failures. Remarkably, there are times when he is regarded, and abused, as both simultaneously.

When he appears to be in the shadow of a dominant Secretary of State or other senior government leader, he will be chided for being weak and sterile. In eras when his role seems less submerged, he will be attacked as a power center beyond the reach of party shifts. It is then alleged that his baleful influence continues even as presidents and secretaries of state come and go.

And although a career official, the diplomat often finds himself brought into domestic politics. This is especially true in the United States, where the combative state of executive-legislative branch relations is a permanent fixture on the Washington scene. But it happens elsewhere as well, and it is not at all surprising, given the importance of the work in which he is involved, and the continuing need for "expert" support for administrative policies coming under legislative scrutiny.

It can be argued that appearances before the legislative committees should be handled exclusively by an administration's noncareer officials, that is, its political appointees. In many systems, including that of the United States, it simply does not work that way. When the career diplomat is caught in this cross fire, his first loyalty, of course, is to the President and to the executive branch, of which he is a part. But it can be an unfortunate situation indeed where the controversy is particularly intense and both branches in effect have a veto over his future career.

There are other occasions when a diplomat may find himself facing risks of a quite different character. Unfortunately, the threat of kidnaping, murder, and other forms of terrorism, while fluctuating from era to era, is never totally absent from the diplomatic scene. Anyone who has had responsibility for dealing with these problems can never forget the quiet courage of those who were saved and those who were not.

A notable example of the latter were Cleo Noel and Curt Moore, captured and brutally murdered in Khartoum in March of 1973. Both highly respected career diplomats, Noel was the newly arrived American ambassador and Moore, his long-time friend, was the departing American chargé d'affaires. They were captured by terrorists while attending a farewell reception given in Moore's honor by the Saudi Arabian ambassador. In the long hours that followed, all rescue attempts proved unavailing, and Noel and Moore were told by their captors to prepare for their "execution." After writing farewell notes to their wives, and as they were being led to their vicious, senseless murder, they paused to console their stricken host. Gently they thanked him for his effort to honor Curt and for his generous hospitality. Moments later, in a hail of automatic weapons fire, their assassins' work was done.

Courage, it is said, is grace under pressure. It is hard to think of a finer example.

It was approached, perhaps, a few days later when two widows began their lonely homeward journey. Sudanese troops and large crowds of Sudanese and foreign friends were awaiting them at the airport to do them honor and to say goodbye. As they stepped from the embassy limousines to the airfield tarmac, a Sudanese military band broke into the haunting strains of "Auld Lang Syne"—played in slow march time, over and over again, as long as they remained on Sudanese soil. Determined that their conduct should be a credit to the husbands they had lost, they, too, never faltered. And they, too, comforted sorrowing friends as they slowly made their way to the plane which the President of the United States had sent to bring them and their husbands home.

Accompanying them on that sad journey, and flying just ahead of a second American plane carrying the body of a Belgian diplomat who had also lost his life in the same grim episode, I found my thoughts turning to cookie pushing and other characterizations of that ilk. In such circumstances these become something more than bad caricature. They become an obscenity.

It is the host country's responsibility to protect diplomats accredited to it. All diplomats know, however, that there can never be a full answer to this problem, either through the efforts of the host government or through the added help of their own. Nevertheless, the threat can be reduced by following a twofold strategy. First, all practical steps (and there are a number of them) must be taken to increase the physical risk to political kidnapers and murderers. Second—and in the end this is the key—the rewards to terrorists must be reduced to zero.

This means under no circumstances paying any tribute or ransom. It is a hard policy, but to follow any other is simply to encourage the spread of this vicious tactic. When universal international conduct reaches the point at which all nations without exception bring to justice outlaws of this kind, it may become possible to act somewhat differently. In domestic criminal—that is, nonpolitical—kidnaping situations in the United States, ransom is often paid, but that is because the quality of our domestic law enforcement is such that the ransom is usually recovered and the culprits are almost always brought to justice. When a similar point is reached in the international scene, a no-ransom policy can be reexamined. Until then, no other makes sense.

Many diplomats understand this, even if some of their governments do not. What is far more difficult for the diplomat to accept are the measures taken to implement the first half of the strategy—increasing the risks to the terrorists. This can involve the inhibitions of armed guards and reduced exposure to the public places and private citizens of the country to which he is assigned. As these are among the principal rewards of diplomatic life, their curtailment is keenly felt.

Perhaps the most longstanding and certainly some of the most difficult hazards faced by the diplomat are those made inevitable by the very nature of his business. A diplomat by definition deals with foreign affairs. This means he deals not only with his country's interests beyond its borders, but also with foreign nations' interests beyond their borders. Any nation can unilaterally decide the former, but not the latter—and somehow diplomats are often held accountable by their fellow citizens for other nations' having minds of their own. Even when there is recognition that the minds-of-their-own problem exists, it is not always understood that even in similar circumstances other minds can react quite differently because of different traditions, backgrounds, and concerns.

Objectively analyzing and explaining other nations' goals and viewpoints is a basic duty of the diplomat, for information of this kind is essential to any sound process of foreign policy decision making. Again, this often makes trouble. It can be taken, and mistaken, by officials elsewhere in his government for an overly solicitous interest in the objectives and feelings of foreigners. The result is a suspicion within his own government that he is not to be fully trusted with the interests of his own countrymen—a taint which can plague him throughout his career.

Still another problem stems from a characteristic of democracies which de Tocqueville identified long ago. Referring to the conduct of foreign affairs, he noted, "There is a propensity that induces democracies to obey impulse rather than prudence and to abandon a mature design for the gratification of momentary passion." It is the unpopular duty of the diplomat to stand always against the tide of passion. He must battle for logic in situations where others, wittingly or unwittingly, are determined that logic will not prevail.

Perhaps the most galling of all problems for the diplomat, closely related to what has just been said, is the need so often to be cast as the negativist and faint heart. Not all criticisms on this score are invalid. Unfortunately, far too many diplomats appear as they grow older simply to be learning more and more reasons why more and more things won't work. They forget that their job is to define opportunities as well as risks. Nevertheless, the latter is a critically important aspect of the diplomat's job, and if he pursues it responsibly, it is bound to cause him difficulty.

Most people in most countries put relations with other countries out of their mind until a crisis or serious problem begins to emerge. It is the irritating duty of the diplomat to draw attention to these problems and to the difficult choices in advance, an often unwelcome role. Moreover, it is sometimes his unpleasant responsibility to explain to senior officeholders why their bold and imaginative new proposals are impractical. As a result, the diplomat will often find himself unpopular, not only with the public or with Congress, but, because of his "unresponsiveness," with his own immediate chiefs as well. Unfortunately, the requirement to be responsible and the duty to be unresponsive often go hand in hand.

§

Change, animosity, misunderstanding, and lack of appreciation are hallmarks of the diplomat's lot, as even this abbreviated catalog of diplomacy's hazards reveals. Such problems are hardly unique to diplomacy. They plague most human activities of consequence. In any event, they are a small price to pay for the extraordinary compensations and opportunities that are waiting in diplomatic life. For the plus side of the ledger is impressive, indeed.

By any standard a diplomat's life is broad-gauged and stimulating. It requires constant familiarity with the main currents of life in his own country, as no diplomat who loses touch with these can be effective. It exposes to him as well a wide variety of other currents flowing through other lands. It is a job which brings him in continuing touch with many stimulating public officials and private citizens both at home and abroad. Moreover, if he is operating under a sensible assignment policy, he will have rewarding opportunities to live in fascinating lands without, as in earlier times, running the risk of becoming a permanent exile from his own. Based on these considerations alone, it is a rich and rewarding profession.

It is also a profession with room at the top. Most institutions are organizationally structured as a pyramid, with positions toward the peak severely reduced. In diplomacy, the organizational structure has a marked bulge at the top. Few other institutions have, in proportion to their size, as many important "vice presidencies." If the Secretary of State or Foreign Minister is the equivalent of other institutions' presidents, then surely ambassadors, deputy chiefs of missions at senior embassies, and consuls general—and at home under secretaries, assistant secretaries, and in many instances deputy assistant secretaries—are the equivalent of important vice presidents. In the case of the State Department, because of the size of the international community with which the United States deals, these senior positions run in the hundreds, while the departmental staff as a whole is one of the smallest in our government.

It has become fashionable in recent times to belittle the responsibilities of many diplomatic jobs, including some of those just cited. It is true, of course, that some of these operate where our interests are limited. It is also true that many other government officials besides diplomats now have responsibilities in the foreign affairs field. But given the world as it has become, the diplomat's work is surely more important than it has ever been. In fact, it can be argued that a number of country desk officers in the State Department now have a greater responsibility with respect to peace and war than did many secretaries of state not so many years ago.

Then, too, diplomacy provides those enormous satisfactions that can only come in a life committed to the service of others. The diplomat's first duty is to advance the interests and above all guard the security of his fellow citizens. He is a front-rank, lifetime soldier in his nation's effort to survive and to succeed in a violent, predatory, combative, and unstable world. A life devoted in this way to the service of his countrymen carries its own rewards.

There is an additional responsibility of unique importance, entirely consistent with this paramount duty to country, but reaching beyond it, and shared with all bona fide diplomats everywhere. This is the collective obligation of all true diplomats to work for the cause of peace. It implies no lessening of zeal in the pursuit of national interest. But it requires a concurrent lifetime commitment to the dismantling of situations which lead to war, to the strengthening of the processes for peaceful change, to the strengthening of the fabric of fair and peaceful settlements.

In sum, diplomats, regardless of nationality, have an enduring obligation to their guild and to each other to work always toward that most elusive of human objectives—a just, universal, and enduring peace. The opportunity to spend a lifetime in this effort constitutes the final overriding affirmative of the ledger we have been discussing.

Many operatives on the diplomatic scene, masquerading as diplomats, recognize no such obligation to maintain the peace, and shortsightedly function as if it did not exist. It is, however, a commitment which all true diplomats honor. It is what elevates their profession. It is what makes it the angels' game.

§

It is a game, however, which can afford no illusions. It is played in a hostile, complex, and scarcely angelic environment. It is played in an environment where wishful thinking, sloppy thinking, miscalculation, or other forms of inept diplomatic performance can be suicidal. This is so not simply because of false colleagues or because all nations, like the human beings from which they stem, can be swayed by illogic, ambition, insecurity, selfishness, self-righteousness, anger, greed, recklessness, and an itch for violence.

More critical still is the fact that peace is not the number one objective of any nation. All nations, for example, put the maintenance of their independence, and securing the basic essentials of life, ahead of peace in their priorities; and history is replete with instances when nations (or their leaders) sought war for far more selfish and less defensible reasons. Peace in such a world cannot be achieved by simply wanting it—a fallacy which has plagued us from the beginning of time. For there is always something that is wanted more.

When war comes it represents the ultimate failure of the diplomat. In failure, however, his responsibilities are not at an end. He must seek to contain the fighting and bring it to an acceptable conclusion as soon as possible. Equally important, he must seek, often in the face of much-diminished influence, to guide events in such a way that postwar conditions will not undermine a future peace.

CHAPTER THREE

The Core Qualities

N0 DIPLOMAT CAN TODAY BE effective, nor lay legitimate claim to the title, unless he has mastered the personal "core qualities" and the professional "core skills"—old and new—which the modern profession requires. Otherwise, no matter how deeply committed he may be to his country's interests and to the cause of peace, he is taking his salary under false pretenses. Not only will he be ineffective in any positive sense, but he can on occasion be a menace on the international scene.

There are four necessary personal core qualities and the first of these is integrity. "Whatever the qualifications of a modern diplomat," Charles Thayer has written, "the art of deceit is certainly not one of them." For in the long run, to be successful a diplomat must, in the words of Jules Cambon, "be a man of the strictest honor if the government to which he is accredited and his own government are to place explicit confidence in his statements."

Integrity is not a quality which, in the public mind, has universally been ascribed to diplomacy—and often with good reason. "If we had done for ourselves what we have done in the name of Italy, what scoundrels we would be" is Cavour's purported phrase. And the tactics and morals of Talleyrand and Machiavelli have never been regarded, and rightly so, as mere aberrations on the diplomatic scene. In some eras duplicity has appeared a far truer characteristic of the profession than integrity, and in all eras there has been an abundance of Talleyrand-Machiavelli-type operatives who have regarded it as their duty to seek advantage for their country by the employment of any means, fair or foul.

The debate in diplomatic literature over the relative efficacy of artful deception versus integrity has been a long one. The "patriotic lie" has been defended, and Machiavelli's words on diplomatic promises will always have their adherents. Such promises should not be honored, he wrote, "when their observance is contrary to [the prince's] interest and when the causes that induced him to pledge his faith no longer exist." Apparently recognizing the vulnerable nature of these words, Machiavelli goes on to explain that, "If men were all good, then indeed this concept would be bad, but as men are naturally bad and will not observe their faith toward you, you must in the same way not observe yours to them; and no prince yet lacked legitimate reasons with which to color his lack of good faith." Years later Stalin is said to have put it more simply. "Promises are like pie crusts," he is alleged to have commented, "made to be broken."

But Cambon has long had impressive allies. More than two hundred years earlier, de Callières wrote the classic rebuttal to this amoral concept of acceptable international conduct. "The good negotiator," declared de Callières, "will never found the success of his mission on promises which he cannot redeem or on bad faith. It is a capital error, which prevails widely, that a clever negotiator must be a master of the art of deceit. Deceit indeed is but a measure of the smallness of mind of him who employs it and simply shows that his intelligence is too meagerly equipped to enable him to arrive at his ends by just and reasonable methods. No doubt the art of lying has been practiced with success in diplomacy; but unlike that honesty which here as elsewhere is the best policy, a lie always leaves a drop of poison behind, and even the most dazzling diplomatic success gained by dishonesty stands on an insecure foundation. . . ." And later in the same treatise, he writes, "Beyond the fact that a lie is unworthy of a great minister, it actually does more harm than good to policy because, though it may confer success today, it will create an atmosphere of suspicion which will make success impossible tomorrow. . . ." And again, "In general it should be the highest aim of the diplomat to gain such a reputation for good faith that both at home and abroad they will place reliance both upon his information and upon the advice that he gives."

Writing approximately one hundred years later, Lord Malmesbury, whom history associates with less scrupulous standards and methods, in his famous letter to Lord Camden, nevertheless endorsed these sentiments. Coming as they do from a diplomat whom his contemporary, Talleyrand, termed "the greatest minister [foreign envoy] of his time," his words have a special interest. In 1813, after much diplomatic experience, he wrote, "It is scarcely necessary to say that no occasion, no provocation, no anxiety to rebut an unjust accusation, no idea however tempting—of promoting the object you have in view—can need, much less justify, a falsehood. Success obtained by one is a precarious and baseless success. Detection would not only ruin your own reputation forever, but deeply wound the honor of your court."

Morality aside, it just does not pay to be deceitful. The short-term benefits occasionally garnered by such a practice are outweighed by the consequences of discovery—and in the end there is nearly always discovery. As so many writers on diplomacy have pointed out, a reputation for lack of integrity will follow a diplomat around the earth, and once appended to him he will be suspect at all capitals and his usefulness will be ended. He cannot function unless every day he performs each task in a way which will continue to merit the confidence of both his host country and his own. A true diplomat will cultivate and guard nothing more zealously than a reputation for honorable dealing.

This is not something achieved simply by good intentions. It requires persistent and affirmative professional care against inadvertently misleading governments, his own and his hosts', through the natural tendency to put things to them in as palatable a manner as possible. It requires far more than simply not telling a falsehood. A diplomat does not need to tell all he knows to his host government, but he must never allow his silence to mislead.

No government can expect its diplomats to have powers of infallible prophecy. If they had such powers, they would be likely lost to race tracks in any event. But all governments have the right to expect something more than the elaborately hedged on-the-one-hand-on-the-other-hand predictions which plague so much diplomatic reporting. These are what Sir Harold Nicolson has termed "moral inaccuracies," and many officials fall prey to those who would never consider telling an outright lie.

There are always nimble and treacherous operators on the diplomatic scene who are fully prepared to lie—who will consider it a patriotic act to do so. So the true diplomat, while rejecting this tactic on both moral and practical grounds, must always be on guard against it.

And should the suggestion of an unprincipled action ever emerge from an official of his own government, he must be ready always to repeat the classic refusal of Monsieur de Faber who said under such circumstances to the all-powerful Mazarin, "Monseigneur, you will find many men ready to carry false messages; but you have some need of honest men to speak the truth. I beg you to retain me for the latter."

Finally he must see to it that all nations, including his own, that would not advertently break a commitment do not do so inadvertently through the cumbersome complexities and impersonal unresponsiveness of modern bureaucracies. The world community cannot function if international commitments are not honored, and inadvertent breaches are as subject to this rule as are those of a more calculated nature.

A diplomat then must be a man of integrity in his dealings with his hosts and his own government. Without this quality in the relations between states, the world can never hope to become a more decent place, and in any event this type of dealing has proven time and again to be the more effective. But he must always be on his guard. Deceit and bad faith remain very much on the scene, and they sometimes produce short-term advantage. Relations between states are no tea party, and no place for the naïve.

Before leaving this subject, one additional point is in order. It concerns integrity in a different form, which all true diplomats must have within themselves. For want of a better term, it can be called "internal integrity," because for each diplomat it involves not his dealings with others but those with himself. It requires, beyond more obvious manifestations, a burning lifelong commitment to standards of excellence in everything he does. If it is not there, if one encounters a diplomat who is slothful or otherwise deficient on this score, then his integrity in other areas, too, should be immediately suspect.

§

If integrity is the first great personal quality of the diplomat, then discretion is surely the second. Put more bluntly, a key quality of the diplomat is the capacity to keep his mouth shut. It is surprising and depressing how many are wanting on this score.

Discretion is first of all required in a diplomat's dealings with colleagues of other nations. For while the diplomatic community may have a number of common purposes, its members also represent the interests of their governments and have, therefore, conflicting objectives, often of an important character. No amount of personal rapport or shared interests must ever obscure this basic truth. Disclosure of information should be calculated always to advance national interests either in the short or the long term. Carelessness can do serious, often critical, damage to both.

Responsible diplomats will always be guarded in what they say to each other. They know that the constant application of discretion precludes neither cordial personal relations nor many mutually useful exchanges with competent colleagues. Rather than being put off when they encounter this quality in others, they take it as reassuring evidence that they are dealing with reliable and useful professionals. If this quality is not present, a wise diplomat will be warned off, and will take his dealings elsewhere.

A diplomat must also take special care to practice discretion with diplomatic and other colleagues of his own government. Here the "need to know" principle must be zealously adhered to. This means that all sensitive information regarding a particular subject must be confined only to those officials who should be dealing with it and who, therefore, have an obvious need to know. A natural law of bureaucracy almost guarantees that once sensitive information spreads beyond its need-to-know circle, it inevitably oozes into the public domain. Or at least it spreads to a quasi-public domain. From there, of course, it easily reaches the alert ears of those who serve the conflicting interests of other lands.

It is unfortunate that there is no way that a nation can consult fully and frankly with all its citizens. If there were a way this could be done, without foreign ears listening in, it should be done regardless of the sensitivity of the information involved. But unfortunately there is no way this can be accomplished without outsiders being admitted as well. As long as this is so, the need-to-know principle must prevail.

Many diplomats who would not think of being indiscreet in their direct dealings with diplomats of other nations end up accomplishing the same result indirectly either through the oozing process or through indiscretions with the press. While all diplomats recognize the need for the need-to-know principle, too many seem unable to master a psychologically conflicting personal need—namely not to appear "not in the know," especially in the eyes of their professional colleagues and of their friends in the press.

The result is that heads of governments, secretaries of state, and foreign ministers sometimes get so they won't trust their own state departments and foreign offices, and this tendency for some often seems to become increasingly pronounced the longer they remain in office. This in turn results in diplomats in these institutions, and in their constituent embassies abroad, finding themselves not taken into their leaders' confidence, and, on the crucial issues, not properly informed as to what is going on.

This is quickly sensed by the foreign officials with whom they deal, and their effectiveness is soon curtailed. When this happens, diplomats of course resent it bitterly and complain of it endlessly. They rarely stop to admit, or even to consider, that their own lack of discretion has brought this upon them.

Of all the areas in which a diplomat faces the challenge of discretion, none is more important or more difficult than his dealings with the press. Absolutely nothing is more important to a free people than a free press, and its occasional, and admitted, shortcomings can never obscure this basic tenet of free government. But a soundly functioning diplomacy is also important to protect a free people. The difficulty arises because in certain important respects the two cannot be at peace with each other.

The difficulty may stem, in part, from the fact that diplomacy in many of its aspects was developed in an earlier time, before the overriding value of a free press was recognized and before a free press was fully operative.

The root of the problem is that a properly functioning press deals with disclosure and exposure at all times, while the diplomat deals in these terms only in end results. In his dealings along the way to these results, the diplomat has learned that not only are the best results obtained through confidentiality and privacy, but that often results can be obtained in no other way. This is not, of course, a conflict which is limited to diplomacy. The concept of private negotiations of a public result permeates the dealings of institutions and individuals at all levels of a free society.

It is a very real and very important conflict in diplomat-press relations, which neither side can responsibly lose sight of. It means that if both are doing their job, neither will be fully comfortable with the performance of the other.

For a diplomat, difficulties in his relations with the press are further compounded by two quite different circumstances. The first is that despite the discretion which is required of him in dealing with the press, it is often an important part of his job to talk with its members and to supply them with accurate, timely, and useful information. The objective, of course, is to win increased public understanding of the general objectives of current foreign policy efforts, and of the reasoning that lies behind them. This is essential because foreign policies in the end, even those of great merit, will not be credible and successful if a substantial portion of the public does not support them—or, more accurately, if a substantial portion of the public is actively opposed to them.

A vigorous, aggressive press will not be content simply with information the diplomat, for his own purposes, chooses to release. And in the ensuing encounters, in which each side seeks to serve the country's interest, the lines between proper inquiry necessary to the public interest and premature disclosure contrary to the national interest can become blurred and uncertain.

Diplomats are plagued also by a less important and fundamental problem that can, nevertheless, often be a considerable burden. This has to do with the occasional tendency of top administration leaders to overreact to leaks, at least some of which are not very important, and surely not worth all the concern and irritation lavished upon them. Resentment over this is not lessened by the conviction, widespread in diplomat ranks, that some of the worst leaks come not from the diplomats but from the top leaders themselves.

In his dealings with the press, the diplomat cannot, if he is a responsible operative, retreat from its members, nor ignore their key role in a free society. Nor can he forget the conflict of interest which prevails. He must learn to be frank, helpful, and accurate—but never careless and never indiscreet. In his dealings with both the press and other diplomats, he must also remember always that indiscretions come about in part, as well as in whole—that a fragmentary indiscretion can be as damaging as a whole in the hands of an adroit recipient whose business it is to collect and piece together many parts from many sources, thus coming to understand the whole.

As a diplomat rises to more senior positions, he may lose some of his anonymity and begin to get a "press" of his own. This is especially true if he finds himself in a diplomatic hotseat, either at home or abroad.

Most people in public life, in or out of diplomacy, tend at the beginning to get a favorable press, and it can be a heady thing. There is a natural temptation to keep things going in this direction by courting a reputation for being cooperative with the press, and the fact is that few people rise to, and survive in, top positions who are not fairly effective in their dealings with reporters. If a person's role brings him sustained press attention, however, that attention is soon bound to lose its one-dimensional quality. A friend, later to become a presidential candidate, once told me that when he started his public career he could not wait to see all the fine things that would be written about him. After a while, he found himself only hoping what was written would not be too bad. Senior diplomats, who find themselves playing controversial roles, can soon learn what he meant.

Any government official who is to be involved in important undertakings and to play a role of consequence in them is almost bound to receive excessive compliments and excessive condemnation. Neither should be taken very seriously unless mounting condemnation threatens to undermine his effectiveness. At that point he must, with the help of experts, seek to get his objectives and actions placed in a better press perspective.

Courting the press through indiscretions, in these or any other circumstances, however, is highly unprofessional, and will in the end fail to serve even personally selfish purposes. It will surely undermine a diplomat's standing and effectiveness with his colleagues and his superiors, and in the end with the press as well.

§

Energy in the diplomatic sense means stamina and zeal. A diplomat needs both. He must have the physical resources to sustain a fifteen-hour day, day after day, and even more important he must in times of crisis be able to work around the clock without significant loss of effectiveness. Not all diplomats abroad put in a fifteen-hour day, but if they do not, they are simply not keeping up with the job. A professional cannot truly keep on top of the substantive part of his job, and meet his representational responsibilities, unless he is geared to that kind of day.

Of course, long hours doing what you like are far less onerous and wearing than short hours doing what you do not. So early on, a diplomat must make a careful, dispassionate decision as to whether he likes his work, and if not, he should quickly turn to something else. He must be so genuinely fascinated by its substance that he is deterred neither by its many boring, archaic, and silly aspects nor by the prospect of a lifetime of frustrations inherent in dealing with government bureaucracies, his own and those of other states.

He must be fascinated, too, by his fellow human beings. He must not only have a greater than average sensitivity to the feelings of others, but he must also enjoy their company to an unusual degree. For, like effective politicians, a good diplomat must spend most of his waking hours in the company of others. Over a lifetime this can become a heavy burden indeed, unless he has a genuine liking for people. And again like a successful politician, this phase of his life requires notable qualities of energy and drive. In the diplomat's case, these characteristics are often masked behind a professionally calm and detached manner, but they must be there all the same.

There are a number of ways in which a diplomat's physical "staying power" can be enhanced. An effective diplomat discovers and develops the particular devices that are especially helpful to him. For one thing, it is a good idea as a diplomat grows older to train physically for the job with the dedicated regularity of a professional athlete. A meaningful physical training program pursued each day can do wonders for his physical and mental well-being. And as he works an endless day, he need have no conscience qualms over each day preempting an hour or so for this program.

A diplomat also learns early in the game that health and stamina require abstemious self-discipline as far as food and drink are concerned. By the nature of his business, both become hazards, but because the hazard is such an obvious one, most diplomats keep a careful watch on their intake of both.

One of the most wearying parts of a diplomat's day is the portion given over to representation activities, particularly those of a social character. Diplomats, as just noted, tend to have a special liking for the company of their fellow human beings. By nature they tend to be gregarious and enjoy parties. Moreover, because of the people they involve, diplomatic social gatherings are as a rule unusually pleasant and interesting. But as in anything else, there can be too much of a good thing. Nothing can be more deadly than two or three cocktail party-receptions followed by a formal black-tie dinner night after night, week after week.

This burden can be alleviated, however, if at each function a diplomat attends he keeps a specific objective in mind, beyond being pleasant and representative. He should always have someone he wishes to see, something he wishes to say, something specific he wishes to learn. Each function then ceases to be a chore and becomes an opportunity.

Energy also requires zeal. Unfortunately, too many diplomats have for too long been misled by Talleyrand's famous dictum, *"Et surtout pas trop de zèle"*—and above all not too much zeal. In modern parlance this has been translated into the classic advice all diplomats know: keep a low profile, observe, report. Above all don't make waves; don't get involved emotionally, or in any other way. Abroad, such a laconic stance can only mean that much of importance will pass him by. Certainly at home it means he cannot, with such a philosophy, hope to have significant influence within his own government.

"Diplomacy," declared Charles Dawes, onetime U.S. ambassador to the Court of St. James's, "is easy on the head but hell on the feet." To which, in a famous riposte, a former American ambassador to Italy is supposed to have said, "It depends on which you use." But both missed the mark as far as a modern diplomat is concerned. The latter had better use both every hour of the day, day after day.

It is when a diplomat is stationed at home, however, that a *"pas trop de zèle"* philosophy is the greatest liability. In the modern era of intense bureaucratic infighting with all departments of a government battling to exert influence in foreign affairs, a diplomat who is not personally "involved," who does not care, who is not assertive, who adopts a detached attitude and a low-profile role, cannot possibly be effective. He is going to be so run over that his presence and views will be scarcely noted, let alone have an impact.

This is not to say that the modern diplomat should substitute passion for reason—the world is a far too dangerous place for that. But surely he must forgo a passive role. He must care, he must put an indefatigable drive into his work. Especially at home he must be a "take charge" operative whose voice and views are advanced with zeal and determination. John Kenneth Galbraith's experiences in diplomatic life were more limited than Talleyrand's, but he came far closer to the mark when he declared that what diplomacy requires is "the clear-headed, determined operator who knows what should be done and has a strong desire to do it."

§

A last key personal quality is self-discipline. The need for zeal, the need to care, can never override the need for total self-control.

It is not disturbing to see a touch of a temper problem in a very young diplomat. It can in fact reflect the presence of needed reserves of spirit and drive. The same can be said for a certain degree of excitability and impatience. I recall once sitting with Llewellyn ("Tommy") Thompson, one of America's most accomplished professional diplomats, when an able junior diplomat walked by. After he had passed, I remarked on this young officer's maturity and promise, only to be brought up short with the comment, "I hate to see someone so smooth so young."

But if a touch of temper or excitability can be tolerated and even looked for in the very young, there is clearly no place for it in the performance of the mature diplomat. No nation can afford to be represented in important undertakings by anyone who does not have himself under iron control. A diplomat, in his dealings with foreign officials, faces constant frustrations; and gnawing concerns are often an inherent part of those frustrations. In these circumstances, if he has a low frustration tolerance, he is of course a serious liability to both his sending and receiving states. No foreign office or state department should dispatch such an official abroad. At home, no foreign office should tolerate the presence of such a diplomat in the local embassies with which it deals. The home offices of such flawed operatives should be quietly but firmly asked to remove them.

But self-discipline means more than a capacity for calm, and for controlling one's frustrations and emotions under difficult circumstances. Even more important, it means control of one's ego. For, particularly with more senior diplomats, the problem of vanity can be one of the most deadly—the more so because it is a quiet, malignant disease, often unrecognized by those in its grip.

Vanity of the pompous stuffed-shirt variety is not the key problem. It is true that this still mars the performance of certain diplomats who somehow retain the quaint notion that a profession which so long represented royalty should still be treated as royalty. These are relatively few, and the real problem is far more pernicious and subtle than that. It can lead to a diplomat's adhering inflexibly to assessments and recommendations he has made, and to denying to the conclusions of others the open-mindedness essential to objective analysis. Put simply, the value of a diplomat's judgment declines in direct proportion to the degree he permits his ego to invade the processes of that judgment.

Ego can render a diplomat unduly susceptible to flattery; ego can undermine his relationships with host country officials, with colleagues in his own embassy and back home; and ego can corrode his performance in countless other ways too numerous and obvious to mention.

It is difficult to believe, for example, that there are still diplomats who will leave the table when they find that their hostess has put them at a lesser place than they consider their protocol rank requires. These same officials will react in equally foolish ways in other situations where their sensitivities have been similarly offended and where their diplomatic precedence has not been properly deferred to. In all such instances, the invariable after-the-fact rationalization on the part of the offended diplomat is that his objections and actions were based on the affront which had been offered to his country. If he were more honest with himself, he would discover that it was his personal ego which was the real cause of the difficulty.

Quite apart from the fact that it is questionable manners indeed to respond to rudeness with rudeness, the truth is that in almost every case the slight to begin with is an unintended one and the result of human error. In diplomatic life, people simply do not set out to be rude to colleagues or to others with whom they come in contact. And this includes colleagues and others whom they do not particularly like, or who represent countries whose philosophies or policies they do not particularly like. So sensible diplomats should treat any rudeness as unintended and act accordingly. In the rare case where their assumption subsequently proves to be inaccurate, it is still a far more professional way to react than to reply on the spot with an instant rudeness of their own.

Most diplomats, of course, will avoid such flagrant ego trips as the type just cited. Most have their egos sufficiently under control to refrain from far less silly things than this. But no one can be entirely exempt from an ego problem. Experience has shown that even the most self-effacing must be ever on guard against its dangers.

Intelligence—that is, a high order of sheer brain power—in diplomacy, as in anything else, can be an enormous asset, and no one can function effectively in this profession (or should be able to pass the entrance examinations given by all career diplomatic services) without a respectable I.Q. But the needs of diplomacy go beyond this. Above all, they require a disciplined intelligence. This means a mind that each year becomes more orderly, more objective, more able to encompass all aspects of a problem, more informed, and more resourceful.

Most diplomats assume that they have come to their profession with an inherent commitment to each of these critical core qualities of the bona fide diplomat—integrity, discretion, energy, and self-discipline. They soon find, however, that in the stresses and complexities of their profession these qualities are far easier to believe in than to adhere to. Put another way, believing in them on the one hand and instilling them indelibly in one's character and performance are quite different propositions. The latter is an endless task, one the diplomat must pursue from the day he enters his profession to the day he leaves it.

CHAPTER FOUR

Messenger-Reporter: The First of the Core Skills

DIPLOMACY REQUIRES CORE SKILLS as well as core qualities, and paramount among these is the ability to be an accurate reporter. A diplomat must be many things today that he did not have to be years ago, but if he cannot be relied upon to report accurately the views of his own government to his host government, and if he cannot be equally relied upon to convey the views of his host government to his own government, then he does not meet the first qualification of a diplomat. He becomes instead a serious potential liability on the diplomatic scene. Of all the core skills he must master, none is more fundamental.

It is a skill which requires much careful effort to acquire, as all conscientious newspaper reporters will confirm. It means being able to convey exactly what his government wishes to convey to the government to which he is accredited. It means reporting the exact words which he has used. It equally requires an infallible ability to record the exact words which have been said to him in official conversations. And in both cases there must be the ability to assure that the substantive context in which the words are spoken is precisely understood, both during the conversations themselves and in the subsequent reporting of them.

Generally, young officers enter diplomacy underestimating the difficulty of this skill. After some years of experience, however, they learn to recognize its complexity and eventually to master it to an impressive degree. If they are not careful, however, they may find, in one key area, that mastery slipping at a later crucial period in their career.

For as they become more senior and come to deal with more influential foreign figures, their conversations become increasingly important and are reviewed with increasing care by the top officials of their own government. Conscious that their "readership" will include presidents and secretaries of state occasionally, and officers and officials just below that level regularly, there is sometimes a temptation, understandable but unacceptable, to emphasize professional competence at the expense of absolute accuracy. Thus, some senior diplomats never appear to come out second best in their conversations with host country kings or presidents or with their prime ministers, foreign ministers, or other senior officials. In fact, if all conversations at that level were as adroit, deft, and persuasive as some reporting cables would suggest, then surely we would have far fewer problems remaining in the world than we do.

A colleague of mine some years ago, as part of his training, was asked to accompany his ambassador during a call on the chief of state of the country where they were serving. Afterward, the young officer was present as the ambassador dictated his reporting telegram to the State Department. That dictation had not advanced many sentences when my young friend found himself interrupting to say, "But, sir, that is not exactly the way you put it to the king." There was a shocked silence as the ambassador contemplated the enormity of this intervention. Finally, he rallied to proclaim, with exasperation and inaccuracy, the classic rationalization for such unprofessional reporting. "Always remember, young man," he said, "it is not the specific words that are spoken, but the essence of what was said that is important."

In fact, as is so often the case, the ambassador had performed in a highly creditable manner. It was just that, in the reporting, he could not resist making that performance appear to be just a little more adroit than it actually was. Of course, there are many senior diplomats whose integrity and ego control prevent their indulging in any such reporting, but it is a trap which even the most conscientious of reporting officers must be on their guard against.

A variant of this *tour de force* problem in diplomatic reporting lies with the diplomat who cannot suppress his desire to be clever and witty in his reports to his headquarters. This attention-gathering device can often make his reporting more lively, but it carries with it in the long run a considerable threat.

"This man is trying harder to be clever than to be accurate," I once heard a secretary of state say after reading a cable from one of our wittier ambassadors. It was the reaction, too, of his less senior readers. Unless a diplomat, therefore, is one of the very few who are blessed with a dual capability for both accuracy and wit, he should focus by all means on the former and let the latter go. This rule does not add to the liveliness of diplomatic reporting, but it does wonders for its reliability and utility.

Another danger which must be guarded against is the tendency to present unpleasant news either to the host country government or to the diplomat's own government in as palliative a manner as possible. Up to a point this is a valuable and desirable skill in a diplomat's dealings with his host country's foreign office. When it is overdone, however, as it sometimes is, it becomes a form of deception which, of course, must be scrupulously avoided both with the diplomat's own government and with his host government. Governments can be helpful in this process by making clear that they welcome candor from their own and foreign diplomats. As de Callières noted long ago, "The truth requires two agents, the one to tell, and the one to hear."

In addition to integrity, ego control, and a well-developed memory, certain practical devices can be used to help ensure accurate and balanced reporting. The first and best is to show the report, before its dispatch, to the official with whom the conversation was held. Nothing is better calculated to eliminate *tour de force* drafting and to ensure a balanced and accurate report. This device is particularly valuable if, in the conversation being reported, commitments have been made on behalf of either government.

In circumstances where this procedure is not feasible, a responsible diplomat must have the self-discipline still to draft his report as if he were going to show it to the official involved. In the reporting message that results, he may not appear quite as adroit and effective as he would like, but his chiefs back home will have a more reliable and useful report than might have otherwise been the case.

Another excellent device is to take a note taker when involved in an important conversation with foreign officials. This will, of course, again not always be feasible. Some important conversations take place at a dinner, or reception, or in other circumstances where it is not likely that a note taker will be nearby. And, depending on the style of the official and the nature of the subject, there will be other occasions where officials will prefer to speak privately, without any extra persons in the room.

Some senior diplomats resist as a matter of style having note takers with them, feeling it inhibits the conversation (and perhaps subconsciously believing that this practice reflects adversely on their own professional capability). Undeniably, there are occasions when, either because of the intimacy of the setting or the nature of the subject, the presence of note takers is inappropriate. Whenever it is feasible, however, for each participant to have one present, it is a good idea to do so. Then, after the meeting has been concluded, the two note takers can be instructed to review their notes together to ensure that both governments have a similar written record of what was said. This is a useful device even for those conversations where, to ensure clarity, an aide-mémoire has been left or subsequently dispatched covering the basic points being made.

§

Reporting in diplomacy is, of course, not limited to recording and relaying official conversations between governments. The major portion of the reporting performed by diplomats abroad is devoted to keeping their own capitals informed as to what is going on in their host countries. Because there is so much going on, however, it is essential that a diplomat learn to be selective in what he sends to his readers back home.

This means that the capacity to be a discriminating reporter—the second of the diplomatic key core skills—is nearly as important as being an accurate reporter. This has become especially so in modern times when the sheer volume of reporting by the more active diplomatic services threatens to overwhelm their respective state departments and foreign offices.

Overreporting was not always a problem. For most foreign offices, for a very long time, the opposite was the case. "You certainly will not wonder if the receipt of but one letter in two and a half years inspires a considerable degree of concern," wrote Secretary of State Thomas Jefferson to an early representative in Spain; and by 1838 U.S. consular regulations were still reflecting a pace of reporting which was leisurely indeed by later standards. "Counsels are expected," those instructions read, "once in three months at least to write to the Department, if it be for no other reason than that of apprising the Department of their being at their respective posts."

Combine all this with the fact that hazardous travel conditions meant a certain portion of this limited early reporting went astray, and one can understand why few foreign offices had the problem of overreporting. Now, however, with almost instant telegraphic facilities, rapid air pouches, a proliferation of missions abroad, and the deeply rooted belief that voluminous reporting is the key to early promotions, this has become a problem indeed.

Certainly what is not needed today is the stream-of-consciousness reporting which so often inundates modern headquarters with indiscriminate facts and comment of small and large import. What is required instead is a careful focus on only those facts which are of direct and significant interest to the government, and on only those developments which will have a consequential impact on the government's interests. And the latter must be accompanied by a useful analysis of just what that impact is likely to be.

In an earlier period, and in the absence of an international press, envoys sometimes performed a more general news reporting function for their sovereign. This obligation has long since been overtaken. Modern embassies are not newspaper offices and, unlike the *New York Times,* cannot be interested in "all the news that's fit to print."

And just as diplomats are not newspaper reporters who must record all that goes on, neither are they like newspaper columnists who must turn out a piece of analysis each day. A careful report whose focus is not on what has already taken place, but on what is likely to happen in the future to his own country's interests as a result of what has taken place, often requires additional time for careful thought. Its author's silence in the interim will be regarded by any wise foreign office as a double blessing. It means headquarters will be spared the daily diversion of energy required to digest reports of marginal or less value. And it will ensure the type of reporting which, if properly done, is invaluable. A well-known saying among diplomats is that "A report a day keeps the inspectors at bay." In modern diplomacy, however, the exact opposite should be true. A report each day from each diplomat at post should bring inspectors on the scene with a vengeance.

Unfortunately, modern-day diplomats' efforts to be discriminating in their reporting are often undermined by their own governments. The reason is that governments have a difficult time indeed in determining the exact compass of their interests in each foreign country, and in delineating the type of facts which do, and do not, fall within the category of "direct and significant interest." Individual departments within the diplomat's own government may well have very fixed views regarding just what should be reported on and what should not. The difficulty, however, is that there is no consensus of views between departments. The result is that diplomats abroad are confronted with a voluminous and continual flow of requests for reporting—requests of an extraordinarily diverse and far-ranging scope which emanate from every nook and cranny of his government. This, of course, highlights the compelling need for improved systems for establishing priorities with regard to the insatiable reporting demands of all modern governments.

Brevity, consistent with both clarity and accuracy, is a virtue devoutly to be sought by all diplomats. Where achieved, it earns undying gratitude in a profession where eye strain is an enduring occupational hazard. As in anything else in diplomacy, it takes practice, for it is far easier to draft a long report than a good short one. A diplomat can make a start toward this goal if he will adopt the practice of reviewing everything he writes for the purpose of ruthlessly eliminating every adjective not absolutely essential. Not only will this shorten the draft, it will do much for its clarity. As Sir Ernest Sato advised earlier generations of diplomats, the use of an adjective which can be spared "only weakens the effect of a plain statement."

Nevertheless, and as in anything else, brevity can be overdone. An illustration that comes to mind is a two-sentence telegram allegedly once sent by a long-ago American ambassador to Cairo. "Today," that message is said to have read, "the Foreign Minister told me that the government of Egypt was considering making war on the Sudan. I told him it better not." While brevity is always to be desired, so in this type of situation would be the ambassador's views as to whether the remark of the foreign minister was a serious one and what in fact were the prospects of a war between those two countries.

As a concluding point in discussion of these first two major core skills, it is perhaps worth emphasizing the obvious; namely, the reporting duty places an awesome responsibility on the diplomatic profession. It demands from the diplomat a performance which is devoid of all that is casual, imprecise or slipshod.

In this connection a senior colleague once told me that he regretted the passing in the American diplomatic service of the requirement that all dispatches to Washington begin with the phrase "To the Secretary of State: Sir, I have the honor to report. . . ." It was not that he was especially enamored of this archaic salutation, but rather that he was convinced that when a diplomatic officer in earlier times had to begin his report in this manner—and even though it was known even then that secretaries of state could not possibly read all that was addressed to them—this evoked in the reporting officer a salutory sense that the words which followed must be prepared with the greatest of care to assure accuracy, relevance, clarity, and brevity.

Be that as it may, the point to be underscored now is that in modern reporting these critical requirements are still there, even if the salutation, which my colleague thought so valuable, has long ago passed to the limbo of forgotten things.

CHAPTER FIVE

The Art of Negotiation

SIR HAROLD NICOLSON HAS WRITTEN that diplomacy "is a written rather than a verbal art" and more precisely that it "is not the art of conversation, it is the art of negotiating agreements in precise and ratifiable form." While this understates the importance of the verbal elements of diplomacy, there is no denying that nothing lies closer to the heart of the diplomatic process, or is a more important part of it, than the reaching of written agreements between states.

It is particularly unfortunate that the systematic development of this core skill is one of diplomacy's most neglected areas. In some assignments, a diplomat may find that he is heavily involved in continuing negotiations of one kind or another. Often, however, he may go for several assignments, covering a number of years in his career, without being engaged in a negotiating process of any real complexity or importance.

Over a lifetime, on the basis of trial and error—and on the basis of intermittent but in the end rather extensive experience—many diplomats become very effective negotiators. Because of the sporadic, hit-or-miss, on-the-job character of so much of a diplomat's negotiating training, however, nations often pay a considerable price for his ineptness and inexperience in the long years before he achieves an acceptable level of professionalism.

A negotiator now operating abroad is far less on his own than before. Modern communications provide a guidance and support not previously possible. From the negotiator's point of view this is a mixed blessing. It means a constant stream of advice, some of which can represent an excessive and unwise interference in his efforts. It also means that authority to proceed is often delayed while a cumbersome bureaucracy at home functions ponderously and often becomes bogged down in endless internal argument.

The result is that today's negotiator abroad has to devote far more time and attention to the backstopping effort at home than did his predecessors. And often he finds the frustrations and difficulties present in that process to be far more challenging than those he encounters in the actual negotiations.

Nevertheless, this situation has its clear advantages. Because communications were so difficult, earlier negotiators tended, with some notable exceptions, to be excessively cautious. Their basic effort too often, it seemed, was to guard against mistakes which later could lead to headquarters' opprobrium, and even repudiation. This is no longer a concern, and the negotiating process is the better for it. With modern communications a diplomat can be confident that he will not stray far from the path that is wanted.

Moreover he can have the benefit of the collective negotiating experience of his backstopping team—a valuable asset not available to his predecessors. Unfortunately, this is sometimes not as valuable as it should be. Too often the negotiating training of these team members has also suffered from a too casual and intermittent experience.

The problem is further compounded by the fact that a seasoned and able diplomat—whose negotiating skills have been finally and fully developed—takes all his hard-won experience and ability with him when he retires. Succeeding generations of diplomats are left to start over again, to make the same mistakes, to go through the same costly learning process.

There is no way to make someone an instant negotiator. No senior diplomat can simply transfer knowledge and techniques, developed over a lifetime, intact to the next generation. Certain aspects of this skill can only be learned by doing. Still, much of what has been learned by preceding generations is transferable. And while no two diplomats will ever negotiate exactly the same way, all diplomats, as they develop their own negotiating style, can benefit from the experience of others. But they can only benefit if their predecessors make a systematic effort to pass along that experience.

Although some senior diplomats are very conscious of their teaching obligations in this and other areas, far too many are not. Nor is it an obligation sufficiently emphasized by the leaderships of the world's diplomatic services.

Of all the teaching responsibilities of senior diplomats, none is more important than the techniques of negotiation. When a senior diplomat is engaged in negotiations, he should ensure that all younger officers in his embassy, or in his office in the foreign office if that is where he is operating from, are involved, even if only as student-spectators. He must take the time to discuss the range of strategy and tactics available to him and the reasons why he chooses the ones he does. He should ask them to join him both in the preparations for the negotiating sessions and in evaluating the results. This process comes hard, however, to many senior diplomats, pressed by overburdened schedules and conditioned throughout a lifetime by the inhibitions of discretion and the need-to-know principle.

Even when he is not engaged in a negotiation, a senior diplomat should continually discuss negotiating strategy and techniques so that the teaching process will go on regardless of whether a negotiation is in process. This and the involvement of juniors in actual negotiations can be a time-consuming effort, but it is an essential investment in the future competence of those who come after.

State departments and foreign offices must also borrow a leaf from the military and set up artificial games—not war games, but negotiating games. Real negotiating situations can be simulated, objectives set for both sides, and evaluations made as participants move through the various rounds of what can be a highly instructive contest. Again, such exercises cannot produce finished negotiators. But they can reveal shortcomings at a time when no damage is done, and they can supply valuable experience during those periods when a diplomat is not learning from the real thing.

Tenacity and persistence are essential qualities of a good negotiator. Rigid stubbornness, which takes no skill whatever, is not. "To negotiate," as Napoleon once said, "is not to do as one likes"—and many negotiators have failed because tenacity was not joined with resourcefulness. The latter is the key quality of an effective international bargainer.

Negotiations are not exercises in charity. Their purpose is to produce a clearly advantageous result for the side the negotiator represents, and no negotiator must ever be allowed to forget this. But there is more to it than that. They should also produce a result that will last.

The consummate art of the diplomat is to negotiate an agreement which is not only to the advantage of his side, but which contains sufficient advantage to the other side that the latter will wish to keep it. Again, de Callières's words have a validity undiminished by age. There is no durable agreement, he tells us, "which is not founded on reciprocal advantage, and indeed a treaty which does not satisfy this condition is no treaty at all, and is apt to contain the seeds of its own dissolution."

Privacy in the negotiating process and precision in the wording of the results are two more essential keys to successful negotiation. For diplomats, Woodrow Wilson's famous dictum must be amended to require "open covenants secretly arrived at," for it is in private sessions that the normal give and take of the negotiating process can best proceed. In fact, as was suggested earlier, it is generally the only kind of forum in which it can possibly succeed. If a party to a negotiation refuses to negotiate privately, therefore, it is fair to conclude that interest in a serious negotiation is absent. His goal instead is one of public relations and propaganda.

On the other hand, a serious negotiation which results in an agreement sufficiently imprecise in its wording to mean different things to the parties concerned means that the negotiation has produced misunderstanding rather than agreement. Such a result can leave the parties worse off than if there had been no negotiation.

There is no single best method or style of negotiating and no two negotiators ever proceed in exactly the same way. Good negotiators have in common an ability to assess their opponents—that is what their adversaries' real objectives are, how they think, what agreements will appeal to them, what will not, how their confidence and respect can be gained if they are decent men, and how the latter can be accomplished even if they are not. They must design opening and fallback positions with great care, to build both mobility and flexibility into the negotiation process, if this should be needed to avoid sterility and stalemate, and to assure that this flexibility will never go beyond the point where national interests are disadvantaged.

In playing out this tactic, Lord Malmesbury wrote to a beginning diplomat of long ago that a negotiator should "make a firm resolute stand in the first offer you are instructed to make, and, if you find this nail will not drive ... bring forward your others most gradually and not, either from an apprehension of not succeeding at all, or from an eagerness to succeed too rapidly, injure essentially the interests of your Court." It is still excellent advice. The timing of the moves in a negotiation is as important as their content. The more experienced a diplomat is in negotiations, the better should be his timing.

Each diplomat through the years must develop his own technique of negotiating. In doing this he must take into account his own personality and then build from a judicious borrowing of techniques of others which he has found to be most effective and suitable for him. And each year, as this process goes on, he should be able to sit down and explain to himself in what specific way he is a better negotiator than he was twelve months ago.

Because no two negotiations are exactly alike, a diplomat must sometimes adjust his techniques to meet special circumstances. When at long last a diplomat's style has become professionally matured, however, this should be done neither often nor lightly.

Many diplomats view with considerable reservation the practice of foreign ministers' and heads of governments' negotiating directly with each other. Nicolson, writing when this practice was far less common than it was to become, was eloquent in his opposition to it. The essence of his case is that neither the environment which surrounds such meetings nor the time pressure under which they operate is conducive to sufficiently thought through or sufficiently precise results.

Summit meetings are here to stay, nonetheless. Chiefs of government are increasingly and directly involved in the management of foreign relations, and modern transportation makes such meetings easier. Foreign relations are the part of the job which often seems to interest leaders most. They enjoy it, and they generally and correctly believe that personal associations of world leaders, and the better understandings of one another which result, can be invaluable—invaluable with respect to both problems of the moment and problems of the future.

Up to a point, however, the concern is valid. It is not that leaders cannot be capable negotiators. On the contrary, it is hard to think anyone could reach these positions without having gained considerable negotiating experience along the way. It is rather that the environment of which Nicolson speaks—that is, the hoopla, the courtesies, the ceremonies, the state dinners, the press interviews, and the shortness of time—is not conducive to careful negotiations and unhurried judgments.

Also, when a head of government becomes directly involved in summit negotiations he violates one of negotiating's more useful rules. The rule is that the official with final authority should not be the negotiator who is in the room and at the table. Regardless of a negotiator's ability, the best guarantee that a calm and measured judgment will be applied to major developments in a negotiation is the requirement that they be referred to higher authority before being finally agreed to. Such a process provides time for the negotiator and his staff, and his higher authorities, to have a last careful review of critical steps before they are finally and formally agreed to. This key protection, normally built into the negotiating process, is sacrificed in negotiations at the summit. Moreover, failure at the summit, if the negotiations are critical, can have uniquely disastrous results. Failure is always more serious if no higher recourse is left.

The remedy for such dangers, however, is not difficult to find. It lies in ensuring that such meetings take place only after the most careful and thorough preparations, and only after whatever agreements are to be consummated at such meetings have been largely worked out in advance.

This in no sense represents an effort to take presidents and secretaries of state out of the action. In all important matters, they will still be making the decisions, but they will make them in circumstances where thoroughness and thoughtfulness are somewhat easier to achieve.

Of course, a situation may arise where immediate, even if un-prepared, high-level discussions, face to face or by telephone, are essential. But at other times, chiefs of government may be determined for less defensible reasons to proceed to such encounters without adequate preparation. Even though diplomats cannot dictate to their chiefs, it is their duty to point out the pitfalls of such a course and to recommend emphatically against it.

CHAPTER SIX
Objective Analysis and Other Skills

No DIPLOMAT BEGINS THE DAY believing that he will allow prejudice, superficiality, or frustration to affect his judgments. Nevertheless, far too many do allow these factors to influence their performance, often without being conscious of it. Years of practice and discipline, aided by the unyielding standards of demanding superiors, are the only answers.

No diplomatic skill is more critical than the power of objective analysis. A diplomat must be able mentally to encircle any situation, to examine it from every possible vantage point. He must know how to dissect each problem dispassionately, to identify each of its elements, and to weigh these with complete objectivity in the light of his nation's interests. There is no place in this process for irritation, frustration, prejudice, or any other emotion which undermines objectivity.

Of all the dangers, however, to objective analysis, perhaps lack of thoroughness is the most common. To be dispassionate is not in itself sufficient to guarantee mastery of this skill. Too often, diplomats fail to collect before them all the factors that bear on a situation, and objective weighing of some rather than all the factors involved risks analysis as distorted as any produced by passion or prejudice. And as the life, thought patterns, and governmental processes of nations become ever more complex, thoroughness becomes increasingly difficult.

"The importance of persuading a prince or a minister," noted a distinguished French ambassador earlier in this century, "has diminished; that of understanding a nation has increased...." In a diplomat's context, the term "understanding a nation" means, most importantly, understanding how a nation views its interests. Winston Churchill once said in a well, but incompletely, remembered statement that he could not "forecast to you the action of Russia. It is a riddle wrapped in a mystery inside an enigma...." Less remembered are the words that immediately followed. "But perhaps there is a key," he added. "That key is Russian national interest."

It is an essential task of the diplomat to analyze how, amid inevitably conflicting opinions, his host nation will view its fundamental interests in regard to developing circumstances or a specific event. He must make sound predictions as to how it will act and think as a result, and what are likely to be the effects, pro and con, with respect to his own country's interests and policies. His professional capability must be such that his home office will have confidence that his analysis and conclusions are based on a zealous collection and dispassionate weighing of all, not almost all, the factors involved.

Such analysis cannot be done through contacts limited to, or at least dominated by, the social strata and senior government figures which tend to engulf diplomats in most capitals. Social figures in this group but narrowly represent the thinking of their country. Important as the views of senior government figures are, there is always an opposition viewpoint, at both the national and local level, which is not only different and significant, but more often than not growing in adherents.

This means, of course, that a diplomat must "break out" of the immediate community in which he lives and systematically develop contacts at all levels and in all elements of his capital city. Even more important it requires a determined effort to get away from the capital and to become familiar with what is being done and said and thought in every section of the country.

Keeping in touch with political opposition elements often presents special difficulties. In less sophisticated countries this can be viewed with suspicion and not understood as a normal function of a diplomatic mission. The problem becomes particularly acute in totalitarian countries, but the attempt can cause difficulties in any country. Efforts must consistently be made, nonetheless, to ascertain the thinking of opposition groups. Where, because of special circumstances, it is not practical for the ambassador to do this himself, he should be sure that it is being done by other personnel resources of his mission. This is not only important for information gathering. Diplomacy is not a matter of sentiment, and admiration or lack of it for a particular leadership should not affect such a practice. Governments change and self-interest requires this essential hedge against that eventuality.

Even though diplomats know the importance of broad contacts, the magnetic pull of the capital and its governmental and social upper crusts often proves irresistible, especially for the higher-ranking diplomats. An occasional whirlwind tour out of the city, followed by a quick return to the capital's establishment circles, is the most that many can manage. Analysis with a base of this kind is of limited value.

While inertia may in part be the cause of "capitalitis," the conscientious diplomat inevitably finds his capital duties to be a heavy and time-consuming responsibility. So much that is important and seemingly urgent must be done there that despite good intentions the days slip by. The wise diplomat, therefore, will block out periods on his calendar when he is determined to be out of the capital, or otherwise engaged in systematically broadening his contacts, and then will ruthlessly adhere to this schedule despite contrary pressures.

Even when a diplomat follows such a program, "understanding a nation" remains an extraordinarily difficult task. Critical information often seems hardest to gain when needed most, and even when all the key factors are clearly available, the correct weighing of them requires perception and experience. Nations generally act logically regarding their national interests—but not always. Thus, in any assessment it is difficult to know how much weight to assign to passion, prejudice, or just bad judgment.

The diplomat can, fortunately, turn to several places for help. He has his colleagues in his own nation's embassy and consulates scattered throughout the host country, colleagues whose cumulative access to facts and collective judgment regarding them can be invaluable. While diplomats serving in smaller embassies will not have access to this large personnel network, no responsible diplomat should reach conclusions without at least exposing himself to these assets where they do exist.

Reliable members of the press can also be an informal source for cross-checking analysis and for conclusions. This has necessarily to be a more guarded and careful exercise given the two professions' inherent disclosure-versus-discretion conflict. Both professions, however, have the common task of reaching an objective understanding of what is going on, and their combined resources to accomplish this are often impressive. On a background basis, without involving classified material, and where mutual trust has developed, the diplomat and the newspaperman have often found that a quiet discussion of conclusions, and of the facts and analyses that have led to these conclusions, can be mutually beneficial.

The resident diplomatic corps is also useful for cross-checking the completeness and balance of analysis and conclusions. Despite differences of interest and objectives, this group, too, has the common objective of understanding a nation and represents an invaluable resource of collective knowledge and judgment.

The diplomatic corps is a club to which each diplomat automatically gains membership upon arrival at post. His relationships with it are something to which he must devote considerable care. Membership in itself does not automatically mean acceptance, and acceptance is important if its knowledge and judgment are to be available to him. Contacts must be systematically cultivated, a not unpleasant task since most diplomatic corps tend to collect an unusual percentage of the interesting and able professionals.

As in any group, however, diplomatic corps' talent and competence are uneven. While courtesy and friendliness to all is a requirement of continued club membership in good standing, it is important to ascertain early on which colleagues, because of their professional capabilities and national objectives, can be most helpful. As with newspapermen, discussions with such colleagues cannot have the same lack of inhibition that would characterize consultations with colleagues within one's own embassy-consulate structure. Nevertheless, diplomats have learned through the years that selective cross-checking with competent colleagues can be invaluable, and for that reason wise diplomats invest considerable effort in cultivating diplomatic corps resources.

This should not, of course, be overdone. Unfortunately, some diplomats, after they have been at their posts for some time, seem to be more comfortable with their colleagues in the diplomatic corps than with the officials and people of their host country. As a result, they appear to make more of an effort to cultivate the former than the latter. In certain closed and authoritarian societies, this may be to a large degree unavoidable, but, even in these situations, it is incumbent upon a diplomat to make sure that time and energy are not unduly diverted to the diplomatic community at the expense of other, more fundamental, responsibilities.

And finally, of course, the point must be made that no diplomat worth his salt will allow any outside resources to become a substitute for his own independent analysis and judgment. If he does, he is a plagiarist, not a diplomat.

§

A mark of a professional in diplomacy is his mastery of foreign languages. In many situations, much of his work, including some of the contacts just discussed, can be significantly inhibited by the inability to communicate in foreign tongues.

Fortunately, unlike some of diplomacy's other key skills, this is an area where many diplomats and many of their parent organizations have focused careful and systematic attention. In most diplomatic services, accomplishment has not yet reached adequate levels, but the effort is there and with time, and somewhat more generous budgetary support, the job will be done.

Some diplomats seem to learn a new language as easily as they take a deep breath. Others must doggedly struggle for much less impressive results. But regardless of aptitude, this skill must be mastered, and every professional must, in addition to his own language, be fluent in at least one of the several world languages. He must also learn the language of the country in which he currently serves, if this is not one that he already knows. All this represents a significant imposition in time and energy on a diplomat's career. Without it, however, his effectiveness and his assignability will be severely limited.

§

Diplomacy's core skills tend to overlap one another and become mutually supportive. The capacity to persuade is another case in point. Involved in this key skill is that subtle combination of tact, sensitivity, character, and articulateness which permits a diplomat to gain the confidence of others and consistently and effectively persuade them to his point of view.

It is one of diplomacy's most ancient requirements, harking back to the days of the herald and orator. It supports the negotiating skill but, unlike the latter, is in continuing use, in one form or another, throughout each working day.

As with negotiating, the capacity to persuade is a skill not generally developed with the systematic effort its importance merits, and, as with negotiating, there is no one best way to persuade effectively. Each diplomat must develop his own technique tailored to his own character and style, and built on judicious borrowings over the years from techniques he has seen successfully employed by others. This will not happen, however, through some vague process of osmosis and good intentions, and wise diplomats will therefore consciously hone this skill each day. They will also find it a useful device to make themselves sit down each year and review what specifically they have learned which makes them more effectively persuasive than they were twelve months before.

§

Senior diplomats not surprisingly attach considerable importance to the capacity to react effectively, rapidly, and resourcefully in the face of unexpected situations. A number of times in a diplomat's service abroad he will not have time to seek instructions before he acts or he will be required to make his recommendations to headquarters almost instantly. On these occasions he must have the ability calmly but rapidly to draw on the experience, capabilities, and resourcefulness developed over a lifetime.

His performance will be enhanced if ahead of time he has systematically reviewed in his own mind just how he would react to as wide a range of sudden and unexpected developments as he can possibly think of. An executive-branch witness in preparing for testimony before a congressional committee should first begin by thinking of every conceivable question he could possibly be asked, no matter how far-fetched, and how he would respond to it. A wise diplomat will put himself through a similar process in preparing to deal with problems at his post that are both likely, and most unlikely, to arise.

CHAPTER SEVEN

The Making of Policy

ULTIMATE RESPONSIBILITY FOR THE implementation of policy lies with the professional diplomat. Ultimate responsibility for the selection of those policies does not. This rests with heads of governments, and with the cabinet officers and subcabinet officers who serve at their pleasure. A career diplomat must remember that there is no great constitutional principle that says that he and his colleagues must have a role in policy formulation. Or that he must be listened to by his country's political leadership. His role grows out of logic but it is not a right. It is a role which must be earned by the constantly demonstrated ability to develop sound and creative policy choices, and to make wise recommendations concerning which should be adopted and pursued.

On occasion this role must be earned in the face of considerable difficulty, for heads of government sometimes develop a tendency to distrust their large diplomatic bureaucracies. In any event, they often feel, and sometimes not very privately, that these bureaucratic establishments tend to be cumbersome, unimaginative, negative, professional bearers of bad tidings, and an excessive source of leaks to the press.

On the other hand, the career diplomat has certain obvious factors working to his advantage. He has the benefit of proximity. He operates figuratively, and often literally, at the elbow of his nation's politically appointed leadership. Even more important, he has in his favor the basic desire of administration leaders to succeed, to take the decisions best calculated to be in the nation's interests. To accomplish this, political leaders should wish to turn to the place where they can get the most competent help—and in the foreign affairs field there is simply no place where there is more help available than in the cumulative knowledge, experience, and wisdom of the nation's professional diplomatic establishment.

Often this asset is wasted, or certainly not fully exploited. This is not only because of the prejudices just noted. Too often it is also because of the diplomatic establishment's managerial and organizational inability to get the needed expertise forward to their leaders in both a usable and timely way.

But the initial point to be made is that it is in the national interest for the professional diplomatic establishment to be deeply involved in the policy-making process. It should not be simply confined to its execution.

A key reason lies in the extraordinarily demanding processes by which leaders rise to prominence in any nation's political-governmental structure, and then maintain their own preeminence in this structure. Leaders who achieve a presidency or prime ministership, regardless of their ability or even their previous experience in foreign affairs, face massive preemptions and diversions of their time and energies. These preclude their accomplishing for themselves an exhaustive, in-depth dispassionate analysis of the nation's wide-ranging problems and opportunities in the foreign affairs area. Nor can they develop for themselves the comprehensive set of foreign policy choices which as leaders they must have before them, a difficult, complex, time-consuming next step following from the analytical effort.

Nor is it safe to rely for all this upon a small group of outsiders whom they have brought with them into office and placed either on their immediate staffs or in other close-by positions. Such a group can often bring remarkable knowledge, experience, and insight into the nation's foreign problems. And while they can bring, too, their own prejudices and oversimplifications, they have the advantage of being less under the spell, and less affected by the momentum, of policies too well and too long understood by the diplomatic establishment. This small group can work with the chief executive more rapidly and in greater secrecy. For a time at least, it can be responsible for impressive virtuoso, ad hoc performances. But no such group, no matter how brilliant, can know all it needs to know. If the professional diplomatic establishment remains isolated from the policy process, sooner or later that process will commit serious error, and the nation will be the loser.

In a responsibly operating government, therefore, the professional diplomatic establishment will be constantly preparing analyses and policy recommendations, consistently reflecting the unique resources and professional standards they bring to this task. And administration leaders will be receptive to this effort and place reliance upon it. This means in turn that the diplomatic establishment must work to belie the adverse prejudices of administration leaders concerning it, prejudices which are almost always exaggerated but sometimes not altogether unfounded. And it means that chiefs of government and their secretaries of state or foreign ministers must join with the diplomatic establishment in a constant mutual effort to ensure that means are found to get policy judgments and recommendations to the chiefs of government and secretaries of state in a timely and useful way. "Timely" means that they arrive sufficiently before a decision is to be made to be of value to the policy maker. "Useful" means that they arrive in a form that is concise, to the point, and not watered down into nothingness by the "clearance" machinery through which they have passed. These are two extraordinarily difficult goals given the environment of modern bureaucracy.

The chief of government, his secretary of state, and his diplomatic service must also make a parallel effort to ensure that a smoothly functioning dissent channel exists for the information of senior policy makers.

None of this is to suggest that the nation's elected executive authority can in any sense abdicate its responsibilities to career diplomats who have been elected to nothing. It is simply that this asset should always be tapped, its recommendations should be carefully weighed, and policy makers should not take important initiatives of their own without first being exposed to its judgment.

The need for confidentiality in this process is essential. Policy makers must be certain they are receiving the most frank and honest advice possible, regardless of whether this advice will be popular with powerful groups in the Congress, press, or body politic generally. If a career official must always act on the assumption that his advice may become public, he must also consider whether he can defend that advice before congressional committees and whether it could adversely affect Senate confirmation prospects for future assignments. Advice given under such circumstances may be inhibited. This is contrary to the interests of his chiefs and his nation.

The solution is clear enough. When a policy choice is made, the chief of government and his top lieutenants must take full responsibility for it. That is their function. That is the way any sound system must work. When groups or individuals in Congress and the press or the public demand to know who it was who recommended this or that action, the reply from the executive branch must be firm. The range of alternatives considered should be supplied, along with the reasons why the other alternatives gave way to the one which was selected. But no administration leadership which has integrity, and which wishes to maintain the integrity of the advice it gets, will ever reveal who among its career officials recommended what.

Confidentiality in this process is important for another reason. The leadership of the administration must feel free, after considering the advice of its professionals, to reject this advice and to adopt an alternate course. Administrations will not feel completely free to do this if the fact that they are operating contrary to the advice of their professionals becomes known and can be used against them by their political opponents.

In the dissent channel, the need for confidentiality is equally great. This is not simply to ensure uninhibited comment, but also to ensure that this vitally important mechanism does not likewise become a source of political ammunition for the administration's opposition. Certainly no chief of government nor secretary of state will, understandably, look with appreciation on a dissent channel system which is so insecure that he finds himself reading headlines declaring that members of the career diplomatic service have put themselves on record as opposing a specific element or action of their foreign policy.

This type of thing has actually happened. Fortunately again, however, a practical remedy is available. The mechanism can be set up in such a way that the prospect of leaks is minimal. In the United States State Department, for example, the practice which on occasion has been followed is for the dissenting group or individual to send forward contrary analyses and recommendations directly and personally to the Secretary of State in one copy only and with no other copy being retained. This system has the dual advantage of reducing to a minimum the chances of leaks which neither the Secretary nor the dissenters wish. At the same time, it guarantees that the views will get to the level where they can count the most.

A dissent channel run in this way is one of the most healthy devices that any foreign affairs organization can establish at home or in its embassies abroad. Moreover, because the young have recourse to it, it can often have an important additional advantage for senior policy makers. For it can expose them to ideas which come from thought processes not yet overly inhibited from too many years of learning why too many things won't work. And secondly, for dissenters both young and old, it is a means of moving their frustration on to a much healthier and more useful basis.

For if no regular and organized dissent channel exists, dissenters tend to be basically frustrated by their inability to get anyone in high places to consider their views. If the channel exists, the frustration shifts. Now the dissenter must focus on the often sobering and extraordinarily difficult problem of coming up with soundly thought through alternatives. Frustration is still there, but it is focused where it should be. It is no longer on mechanics, but rather on the substantive complexities which inevitably envelop controversial foreign policy problems.

On the subject of dissent, there remains a final and vital question. That question is what should a career diplomat do when he finds himself in strong and fundamental disagreement with an action or policy decision which has been taken by the administration's leadership.

The answer lies in an understanding of what is, and what is not, involved in the loyalties that all career diplomats owe to the president or prime minister whom they serve.

A career official has continued tenure, regardless of who has won the last election. He cannot be swept off the payroll by a spoils system which in earlier times served as a guarantee to political leaders that all positions in the governmental bureaucracy, from the highest to the lowest, would be manned by loyal followers beholden to them for their appointments. Such a system, with its sweeping turnovers, also guaranteed a devastating and never-ending loss of expertise and continuity. It was gradually and fortunately replaced by the career system.

For this infinitely preferable system to endure and become strengthened, a *sine qua non* is that the nation's political leaders must have confidence that career officials will serve them with the same loyal cooperation and support as would politically appointed followers.

Loyalty means, then, that a career diplomat must never do anything of a public or private character which would in any way undermine the leaders of the government he serves. But it is essential that loyalty must never be confused, either by the career diplomat or the leaders he serves, with anything remotely suggestive of thought control.

On the contrary, if a career diplomat disagrees with a policy he has not only the right to speak up but the obligation to do so. In fact, he is being disloyal if he does not exercise that right. Loyalty, if it requires anything, requires the giving of one's best judgment at all times.

In this process, however, a professional diplomat does not have the luxury of a private citizen. He cannot simply be "against" or be "concerned about" a certain policy. He must not only give soundly thought through reasons why he is against. Even more important and more difficult, he must put forward practical alternatives, along with soundly reasoned arguments why they are preferable to the policy being followed. As already noted, he must do this in a private channel, and it is the policy maker's responsibility to see that such a channel exists—that contrary views do, in fact, get a hearing.

In a system where this can take place, the dissenter's course is clear. He must make his views known no matter how unorthodox or unpopular. He must then realize that no one can expect his views always to prevail, and that once a decision is made it is his duty to support that decision to the very best of his ability, whether he agrees with it or not. This surely involves frustrations, but unless such a principle is accepted, no diplomatic service can operate.

Of course, an occasion may arise when a career diplomat finds himself in such fundamental disagreement with a decision which he in turn regards of such fundamental importance that he cannot, as a matter of principle, support it, and in fact has concluded that honor requires him actively to oppose it. In the case of a mature diplomat, graced with the humility to know that he is not infallible, matters do not often reach this point. But they obviously and legitimately can, and in the relatively rare cases when they do, the responsible diplomat's course is again clear. As a career official, he cannot publicly oppose a policy which it is his duty to support. Sadly, but inescapably, he has no choice but to resign. He then may be honorably free to follow the course his conscience requires.

Needless to say, career diplomats must have a relatively high frustration tolerance in matters of this kind. If they do not, if they find that their conscience is constantly troubled by the duty to support decisions with which they do not always agree, if such inhibitions make them feel untrue to themselves, then they are clearly in the wrong business. Then they should leave the career service and turn to politics. Or they should become teachers or publicists or be active in some other way where the inhibitions of a career service are no longer controlling.

On the other hand, if one can remain a career diplomat and have the patience to live with the inhibitions involved, the compensations are obvious. Professional diplomacy is surely not the only career through which a citizen can participate in the dual effort to advance his nation's interests and to make the world a better and safer place for all its inhabitants. This can be done from every walk of life. But the diplomat's profession clearly places him at a unique advantage. It permits a lifetime devoted exclusively to these goals. And because he spends this lifetime where the action is, it ensures him a continuing opportunity, and a far better opportunity than most, to put forward his ideas where, again, they will count the most.

CHAPTER EIGHT

Guidelines for Policy

IN THE MAKING OF SOUND POLICY, a diplomat's powers of objective analysis must be focused exclusively and unsentimentally on determining exactly where his nation's interests lie, and what courses of action are best designed to advance them.

Many factors, growing out of logic and experience, will be taken into account, factors whose relevance and importance will vary, depending on the situation he is facing.

He will understand, for example, that contrary to what is often said, traditions of national friendship do still count for something in the world, that common ideals and common intellectual and political heritage can often historically impel nations in a common direction. But he knows, too, that national friendships are basically founded on parallelism of interest, that this is a sounder concept than national friendships, that friendships endure in a reliable form only so long as that parallelism endures—not only endures but continues to be clearly recognized by the nations involved.

As a recommender of policy, he must learn early on that self-interest and selfishness are not the same thing, that a policy objective which seeks a too one-sided result is self-defeating and will have little permanence even if achieved. Arrangements between nations endure so long as they are to their mutual advantage to endure. Otherwise, they fester and soon fall into the category of Stalin's famous piecrusts.

If he is from a powerful state, he must learn to contend with the "muscle-bound giant" problem. This is the problem of a larger state being affronted by a smaller one with impunity on the assumption that, for numerous and valid reasons, the larger state will not retaliate. To combat this tyranny of weakness, the diplomats of larger states must find a way to avoid being trapped between only two choices: either dramatically to use their superior force, or to do nothing. In this situation, the choice must often be nothing. What is needed is a carefully devised set of responses graded over a scale of increasing severity, designed to bring pressure gradually and to avoid the "do-too-much" or "do-nothing" predicament.

Diplomats of smaller states have exactly the opposite goal. They must seek to preserve the inhibitions which restrain larger states so that the smaller states will lose as little of their freedom of action as possible. Diplomats of smaller states will seek to deploy power which is not theirs. They do this by exploiting the involvement of larger powers in the same situations where the smaller powers have a direct and paramount interest. Power does not have to be a nation's own to be useful to it.

On the other hand, diplomats from the larger states should have as a major goal the avoidance of situations where their support for smaller powers, or their involvement in any situation, reaches a point where the small power rather than the larger one will determine its course. Too often a small state can impel a larger one into a crisis or war. And perhaps that war will be with another great power who has also given out proxies in the situation which he cannot fully control.

Policy, to be successful, must be tied to a realistic appraisal of the relative power strengths in the situation. Policy which is not supported by commensurate power is inoperative. Diplomats must understand power, not just in the abstract, but how it is specifically made up and how it specifically affects each situation with which they must deal.

Assessing relative power has become a formidable task. In earlier times, and even as late as World War II, any diplomat who could count was qualified to be a reasonably competent judge of relative power on the international scene. He needed simply to add up the infantry divisions, the artillery, the fighter planes, the bombers, the battleships, the destroyers, and so on on each side. To this he needed only to add a judgment as to the relative industrial-economic strength and the relative national morale of each side. Then, having struck a balance, he was in a position to reach a judgment as to the relative power involved, which probably was as valid as anyone else's.

Today, unfortunately, the situation is quite different. Given the sophisticated offensive and defensive weapons systems, and the infinitely more complex and interdependent economies, there is simply no way that a layman-diplomat can become an adequate relative power expert through his mastery of arithmetic. He now must rely far more on experts than was necessary in the past. In order to understand what they are saying to him, however, and in order not to abdicate to them completely, he, too, must have a rudimentary knowledge of sophisticated weaponry and of more complex economies. It is still another added burden which a modern diplomat has, and which his predecessors did not have.

He must bear in mind, too, that power vacuums in international affairs do not remain unfilled, that power imbalances invite aggression. He must learn that wars often start through the miscalculations of the aggressor. These are brought on in turn by diplomacy's allowing situations to exist which mislead potential aggressors. It is dangerous indeed if they conclude that a potential aggression is more likely to succeed than, in fact, it is.

Where force must be deployed to meet limited aggression, he must understand that the objective is to stop that aggression without turning the situation into a major war. Successful small aggressions almost never satisfy the aggressor. They whet his appetite for more. Appeasement of this limited kind of aggression, then, is one of the surest ways to eventual war. Where force is being deployed to meet a limited aggression, however, a diplomat must see to it that policy makers remember that the principal reason the aggression is being met is to prevent the situation from turning into a major war. This means the aggression must be met with self-restraint—that is, with only the limited force necessary to make it a costly exercise and deny its success. It means that there must be firm precautions to prevent steps which will lead to an escalation of the conflict into a major war. This is never an easy task, and certain voices always urge the nation not to fight with half measures or with one hand tied behind its back. Such advice, if followed, however, can lead almost inevitably to the very war that the whole exercise is trying to prevent.

If an aggressor is determined to escalate his effort to whatever level he believes it will take to succeed, then that war is inevitable. But often this is not the aggressor's strategy. Often he is testing the waters, not prepared to go to that extreme, not prepared, in fact, to go beyond an effort of certain definite limits, hoping to achieve his goal with this lesser effort.

If it is essential for world diplomacy to eliminate situations which may invite aggression through miscalculation, it is equally important to prevent power relationships from developing in such a way that an aggression will be invited by accurate calculation. Diplomacy must prevent, therefore, situations in which an aggressor rightly calculates that his aggression will succeed, that the results will be of great benefit and well worth the effort. It can be argued that World Wars I and II started because a series of circumstances combined to invite miscalculation as to ultimate success on the part of the aggressor. But other wars from the time of the earliest conquerers have started under circumstances which produced calculations of success and benefit which turned out to be accurate indeed.

The diplomat must always bear in mind, too, that the making of a sound peace, in the wake of war, requires an eschewing of the momentum, polemics, sloganeering, and the heroic and combative thought patterns which dominate a nation while that war is being fought. The concept that a war can be fought to end all wars is an illusion. But victors, drawing from the same wellsprings of determination and combativeness and competitiveness which have brought them victory, have demonstrated time and again that a shortsighted, vindictive peace can be constructed that will surely end that peace.

In making policy recommendations, a diplomat must also always remember the basic truth alluded to earlier, that all nations, while preferring to live in peace, place certain priorities ahead of peace. If a self-respecting nation's freedom is threatened, it will fight regardless of the odds. If trade or fuel or food or other essentials are denied a nation to the point where it believes its survival is threatened, it will fight again regardless of the odds. And as nations can on occasion be as illogical, selfish, and shortsighted as the human beings from which they spring, they are capable of going to war for far less logical reasons than these.

It is the duty of the diplomat to strive always to prevent such situations from arising, to prevent the selfish and predatory instincts of a nation confronting another nation with a *casus belli* of this kind. Put another way, it is the duty of the diplomat never to get his own country or his adversary's country into a corner from which no escape can be seen. In the long run, the key to peace is for the diplomatic processes of the world to arrange things in such a way that the disputes which arise between nations are losable, that the essentials of national survival are not being denied and are therefore not involved. Where disputes can be kept to a lesser category of conflicting interests, this permits nations on the international scene, similar to citizens within a national scene, to accept defeat, unhappily but nonviolently, and to operate on the assumption that in the long run in the welter of conflicting interests they will win and lose their share. Put more simply, it is the duty of the diplomatic profession to work for a world which deals in negotiable, not nonnegotiable, demands.

This is, of course, extraordinarily difficult. Even on the domestic scene, where power to prevent disorder is much more impressive, we occasionally see the system break down and violence resorted to. And on the international front, the task will likely become more difficult rather than less in a world whose resources are not endlessly available, and where the population bomb must be treated with the same attention and concern as the hydrogen bomb and other super-weapons which join it on the world scene.

Difficult as it is to bring the world of nations to the point where disputes are losable, demands are negotiable, and essentials of national existence appear assured, this must be the basic objective of all bona fide diplomats, regardless of the nation they represent. It is not inconsistent, surely, with their paramount responsibilities to their own nations' self-interest. At the same time it is the essential condition from which peaceful change, the rule of law, and other key ingredients of a peaceful world order must flow.

As a footnote to the subject of nonnegotiable demands, the true diplomat will always remember that it is the mark of a professional that he never deals in such demands in matters of large moment or small; and he gives, where he can, short shrift to those who do. Even in small matters, the world simply works better when the parties to a dispute both leave themselves some room for maneuver.

In this connection, the professional diplomat must always seek to avoid disputes over principle. "If you want a war, nourish a doctrine," William Graham Sumner wrote years ago. It is a timeless truth. For when doctrine or principle enter the picture, the prospects for compromise and conciliation markedly decline. As has been said, God and the devil cannot compromise over the Ten Commandments.

A wise diplomat will seek always to design his nation's policies so that not all its eggs are in the same basket—that, to change the metaphor, it has hedged its bets when this is feasible.

He will bear in mind, too, that consistency and predictability in foreign policy, especially on the part of the great powers, are important ingredients for stable world order. He will not seek to change or abandon policies that are working, even imperfectly or partially, unless he is certain that there is a sound and preferable substitute available. Imperfections and shortcomings are easy to define. Practical alternatives are among diplomacy's rarest coinage.

On the other hand, he must be on constant lookout for one of diplomacy's most serious problems—the problem of momentum, the tendency that almost all nations have to adhere to certain policies simply because these have become the custom. Too often they do not adequately examine whether the circumstances that made these policies at one time correct and successful still pertain.

He must consider, too, whether his nation's public opinion will support, or at least not oppose, the policy recommendations he is suggesting. A policy, to be successful, does not necessarily have to have a majority of the nation's public opinion mobilized behind it. But no policy, no matter how wise and soundly formulated, will be effective if anything like a majority of national public opinion is opposed to it. In the latter instance, the policy will not be effective because, for the rest of the world, it simply will not be credible.

A diplomat must learn to judge which situations require a policy on the part of his nation, and which do not. No country needs to be involved in all the world's disputes, and one important way in which a diplomat earns his pay is to know which disputes to stay out of. Nor is it, despite the need to cultivate supporting votes for the United Nations and for other forums of parliamentary diplomacy, necessary or desirable to cultivate close, intimate relations with all the nations of the earth. As a practical matter, distant and not very active relations can often be quite satisfactory.

The role of "honest broker" in disputes involving other nations is fraught with peril, as all wise diplomats know. It should only be undertaken in situations where the prospective broker has a major national interest of its own in seeing the dispute resolved.

It is fashionable to believe that nations do not have permanent friends, only permanent interests. But even interests can change their character as circumstances change. Thus, no nation should be regarded, or treated, as a permanent enemy. If enmity is pronounced in one era, it must be dealt with firmly and effectively—but without losing sight of the fact that an opponent's support may be crucial on different issues in a later time.

When there is rising tension between nations, effective diplomats make every effort to avoid a breaking of diplomatic relations. Severing relations is a shortsighted way to demonstrate displeasure. When relationships are deteriorating, or have deteriorated, direct diplomatic dealings are needed most. Diplomatic relations are as important with enemies as they are with friends.

No nation can have a monopoly of wisdom respecting the best governmental arrangements for other peoples' stages of political and social development. This must be worked out by the people directly concerned. Diplomats should oppose all outside attempts to play God in such situations.

They will remember, also, that luck plays a part in diplomatic affairs, as it does in human affairs. It often seems that good breaks and bad go in streaks, imparting a certain rhythm to a nation's foreign policy efforts. Be that as it may, the only two things that anyone can know for certain about luck are, first, that it does in fact influence the course of human and national affairs and, second, that sooner or later it changes.

And luck, of course, becomes a particularly important factor when a diplomat is recommending that his nation take certain calculated policy risks. A wise diplomat will avoid risks, calculated or otherwise, to the extent that he possibly can. Unfortunately, however, he knows that this cannot always be done, because factors which control events often cannot be fully ascertained in advance. Even where they can, a diplomat's task is complicated because he must take into account, too, the oft-proven fact in foreign affairs that when logic suggests that something is inevitable, logic is not always controlling. Logical analysis must remain the basis for all sound policy recommendations. Only experience, however, can build in a diplomat a sense of when logic will not prevail, and when he is most likely to be dealing with the illogical instead.

He must learn to judge when pious peace pacts or nonaggression treaties and the like, often popular with national leaders, are a useful palliative to a dangerous and overwrought situation—and when on the contrary they are themselves a serious added danger, as false ensurers of peace.

He must be certain that policy leaders bear in mind that world opinion and moral force are factors that matter in international affairs, and must be taken into account in reaching policy decisions. He must remember, too, that nations in the past, including the recent past, have defied these factors and intervened physically and success- fully in situations where such an intervention appeared to be contrary to both.

If a situation develops in which his own nation's leaders deter- mine that an intervention is necessary, the diplomat will remember that such an action goes better, politically and diplomatically, with company—that is, with other states joining in the intervention. Above all, the diplomat must advise his chiefs that with or without company interventions are always dangerous, that it is always easier to ascertain how they will start than how they will end.

He must remember that it is generally a mistake to involve the prestige of a chief of government in an effort on the international scene, whether of large moment or small, which is not reasonably sure of success. The fact that a leader of this rank has involved himself will, in the short run, be most favorably received by others on the international scene who share his objective. This is especially true when the intercession is directly on behalf of their interests. If the intercession is not successful, the short-term benefit can eventually be replaced by a lowering of respect and influence. As these are com- modities of value on the international scene, diplomats must seek to ensure that they are not squandered needlessly.

In making policy recommendations, the diplomat must often balance short-term versus long-term interests. He cannot foolishly ignore the future, but neither should he sacrifice bona fide short-term benefits at hand for long-term ones which may never materialize.

He must be certain that policy makers never lead the country into believing that major problems will fade after one last effort, one last battle. This is never so, and leads only to subsequent disillusion and cynicism. Problems in the international area will always be there, and the diplomat must do his best to see that there are no illusions in this regard. The fact that the nation at any particular time is facing international problems is not in itself a cause for concern. The time for concern is when the problems do not change. It is when a problem remains too long unresolved that the danger comes.

There are many other considerations that a professional must keep in mind as he develops his policy-formulation skill. The basic point is that each diplomat must, as he goes along, develop a mental checklist of his own, a set of professional guidelines for himself which gradually emerge as his career advances and his knowledge and experience grow.

Such a compilation must never take such rigid form that it makes its author in the end its prisoner. There are no principles in diplomacy, no matter how sound, that cannot be violated if circumstances warrant. If they are soundly constructed, however, there must be a strong presumption in their favor. It is the diplomat's duty to ensure that they are never violated lightly or unknowingly.

§

In all foreign offices there is a tendency as a crisis unfolds for the gap to expand between the experts on the one hand and the senior decision-making "in-group" on the other. The gap between expertise and decision making is a general problem in government, but in the diplomatic field it becomes especially serious in crisis situations. And the problem arises not simply between the career service on the one hand and the senior administration leaders on the other. Often within the professional diplomatic service itself, there is a gap between the relatively junior diplomats on the desk or on the scene, and their more senior professional colleagues who are placed closer to the top decision-making processes of the government.

As a crisis proceeds, the senior in-group tends to get progressively smaller, partly for reasons of secrecy and partly because in a smaller group it is easier to make the rapid decisions that an unfolding crisis often requires. This can be dangerous, however, because it progressively separates those who know from those who decide. Also the factor of fatigue, which plagues the decision-making process in all crises of any duration, becomes more acute as progressively more demands are made on progressively fewer people.

It is not an easy problem to head off. As a crisis unfolds, senior officials clearly have the authority to determine with whom they will deal, and with whom they will not. But diplomats of all ranks must be on the lookout for it, and, wherever they see it developing, alert the decision makers to the dangers.

§

The key to leadership in foreign affairs as in anything else lies not only in having the expertise but in having the ideas. It is essential that diplomatic establishments of every nation understand this. They cannot rely, as many have a tendency to do, on the title of state department or foreign office to assure preeminence among the many government departments and agencies which now also play such an active part in each nation's foreign affairs. Ideas, not an institution's place in the government's overall table of organization, in the end control who leads.

Despite some notable exceptions, new ideas are not generally the long suit of diplomatic establishments. And for this they are often harshly criticized. One hears talk of "intellectual exhaustion," and assertions that for diplomats "the risks always outweigh the opportunities." Even so friendly a critic as Sir Harold Nicolson has expressed concern about diplomats without imagination who become "all keel and ballast without sail."

The criticism tends to be exaggerated and unfair. Many times it comes from persons with short memories regarding the initiatives which have originated in diplomatic circles. It comes, too, from quarters which have an inadequate appreciation for the importance of consistency and predictability in the nation's foreign policies, and which lack sufficient expertise and experience in world affairs to understand why so many shiny new ideas won't work.

Nevertheless, diplomats who are prepared to take an objective look at their profession must concede that the critics have a point. This is in part because diplomats tend on occasion to overlearn the lessons of their experience, and become too rigidly influenced by them. It is in part because established policies and ways of doing things have, as already noted, an ability to develop a momentum of their own, which makes it difficult for diplomats with overcrowded and badly organized schedules to find the time to alter or even to reexamine them. And it is in large part because good new ideas are extremely difficult to come by, and truly creative people are as rare in diplomacy as anywhere else.

The answer lies first of all in each diplomat's resisting the view that he or any individual group within the diplomatic establishment has a monopoly of wisdom on any particular subject. Moreover, a vigorous adversary system must be built into the various levels of the diplomatic structure. By this is meant an adversary/devil's advocate system designed at each step of the way to reexamine, to challenge, and to seek feasible alternatives both to conventional wisdom and to the specific recommendations being put forward.

The installing of such a system can do much to liberate the latent but generally suppressed collective creative powers lying within any organization. But there is an additional, vitally important step which must be taken. This is consciously to open up all diplomatic establishments to outside ideas from the academic, business, and other communities—in fact, from every other area of national and international life from which ideas can come. To deal with immediate crises and short-term tactics, one must have access to the flow of current cables. To think intelligently about the longer-term problems on the international scene, however, does not require this. What is required is judgment, a knowledge of history and of the world's realities, and time to think.

The solutions to many of the longer-term problems inherent in the search for a more just and stable world are now either dimly perceived or not perceived at all. Recognizing this, all diplomatic establishments must further recognize that, just as no individual or group within an organization can claim a monopoly of wisdom, neither can any diplomatic establishment as a whole make such a claim. Each diplomatic organization must go out and get all the ideas it can, from wherever it can. And this requires the installing of an aggressive system which in an organized, persistent, and thorough way keeps in touch with outside ideas, and solicits this outside help.

Neither of these efforts comes easy to professional diplomats. The first, the adversary/devil's advocate device, presents, to a diplomat who has thoughtfully and thoroughly analyzed a problem and firmly made up his mind, extra internal battles to be fought, and a loss of time where dispatch is often of importance. The second, that of openness, not only cuts across a diplomat's innate instinct for privacy and "in-house" confidentiality, but it, too, is time-consuming—and, where the ideas are either unsound or already thought of, time-wasting as well. Taken together, nevertheless, these two devices represent the best means there are to ensure the supply of fresh ideas, and neither should be neglected.

§

The diplomat must ensure not only that all alternatives are surfaced and considered within his own professional establishment, but that administration leaders (who must in the end carry the political responsibility for the policy decisions which are taken) know them as well. It is not sufficient for the system thoroughly to consider all the options and then forward only the one that careful professional judgment deems the best. It is the duty of a diplomat to present to the politically responsible decision maker not only the course he recommends but also all other viable options.

Otherwise, the busy, hard-pressed leader makes decisions without having all the necessary information before him, and the diplomat becomes to a degree a usurper in the policy-formulation process rather than one of its most vital and appropriate supporters.

§

In times gone by, the intimacy between a nation's official representatives abroad and its private commercial interests was often so close as to be highly improper by today's standards of ethical conduct. Queen Elizabeth's ambassador to Constantinople, to take one example among many, was paid not by the British government but by the British-Turkey Company. He was basically in business—a trader—despite the fact that he was simultaneously the Queen's official representative.

Similarly, the first American to be recognized by the Ottoman Empire as officially representing United States' interests was David Offley, a Philadelphian who came to Smyrna (now Izmir) in the early years of the nineteenth century and spent his business life there operating the trading company of Woodman and Offley. When, as the American consul, he died many years later, he was succeeded by other Offley family members who carried on the same dual role.

No one would advocate a return today to practices of this kind, which so obviously risk the intertwining of public trust and private gain. It is regrettable, however, that the impression is now sometimes given that the pendulum has swung too far in the opposite direction. Modern diplomats, it is too often alleged, do not fully recognize their obligation to become directly and personally involved in the promotion of exports and the support of other national commercial interests—or if they do that, they do not accord it a very high priority in comparison with their other professional responsibilities. Critical fellow citizens, representing these commercial interests, sometimes put it more bluntly. They say diplomats do not understand the importance of this effort or the key role they are in a position to play in it, that they are disinterested and basically look down their noses on it.

It is a blanket indictment which will not stand scrutiny. To begin with, diplomats in economic and commercial sections of an embassy or consulate obviously devote a good portion of their working days and nights to this activity, and their assistance to their nation's commercial interests has been invaluable. The records are replete also with instances where diplomats in other sections, from ambassadors on down, have been of critical assistance as well, though the criticism of inattention occasionally takes on a certain validity here. Diplomats not directly assigned to commercial or economic functions sometimes have insufficient interest in this aspect of an embassy's work, and specifically do not always recognize that all officers in an embassy, not only economic and commercial specialists, have an important responsibility in this area.

Given the importance of this effort to the national interest, all embassy personnel must at all times be zealously on the lookout for useful trade opportunities. Personnel in the embassy's political, administrative, informational, and military attaché sections, to take but some examples, have wide-ranging contacts in the local community of a potentially useful commercial character. It is the duty of all chiefs of missions to see that all such assets are actively and conscientiously mobilized—through embassywide committees or other devices—to discover promising opportunities for his nation's exports. He must also ensure that the general knowledge and expertise lodged in these other sections is just as available to support the commercial effort as is the knowledge and expertise of the economic and commercial sections. Finally, he must recognize that because of the level of his entree and contacts, he himself is in a position to be the embassy's most effective "commercial officer." Chiefs of missions, in effect, must see that all sleeves are rolled up, including their own, in support of this effort. For the modern diplomat, the ability effectively to support his nation's export and other commercial interests is a skill of such fundamental importance that it rightfully takes its place with the other core skills.

Having said this, however, some blunt talk on the other side is called for. Diplomats can help support aggressive and effective sales efforts by their nation's commercial interests—they cannot substitute for them. Too often an attempt is made to shift the blame for a nation's poor export performance to its diplomats' "indifference," when in fact, the fault lies in a host of other factors over which the diplomat has no control. He cannot be held accountable for unaggressive or otherwise ineffectual sales forces, noncompetitive products, overvalued currencies, poor follow-on servicing so essential to repeat sales, and other factors critical in any export effort. It is perhaps human for business leaders to ascribe, in good times, all overseas commercial successes to the quality of their own leadership—but, in less good times, to suggest to both Congress and stockholders that failures are the result of the ineffectiveness and lack of interest of their diplomats. But it is dishonest, and dangerously misleading. When exports fall off, what is needed are not diplomatic scapegoats, but a hard look at the real factors responsible.

CHAPTER NINE

First-Rate People, Third-Rate System

THE EXTRAORDINARY INCREASE, both in the complexity of each nation's foreign relations and in the sheer number and variety of officials conducting these relations, has created an important new requirement for the modern diplomat. He must be a highly sophisticated manager and coordinator. In fact this latest addition to diplomacy's basic core skills is so important that it is no exaggeration to say that the senior modern diplomat must now be a hyphenated operative. He must be a manager and a diplomat.

It is not a development the diplomat has welcomed. Historically comfortable with hunch playing, intuitive, lone-wolf activities, and a heavy reliance on personal "feel" and experience, he finds this in conflict with the new requirements of systematically coordinating large-scale operations, and managing and being managed by others. If being a manager had appealed to him, he would likely have chosen quite different work when he was young.

As for becoming an active participant in his own organization's search for new management tools, and for solutions to its managerial problems, here he would instinctively prefer to remain aloof. Traditionally he abdicates to the experts this complex and extraordinarily difficult task. Then belatedly, but uniformly and severely, he criticizes whatever solutions emerge.

This is obviously not good enough. In today's circumstances, diplomats are managers, whether they like it or not. Not managers perhaps in the exact sense of a senior executive in a large department store, but closely akin to it. For, like their colleagues in other managerial walks of life, they must define basic objectives and relative priorities, out of a welter of conflicting claimants, and then marshal what are never enough resources effectively and proportionately behind those priorities—resources which are not adequate even in the large embassies abroad and in the parent organization at home whose size and numbers begin to rival many outside managerial challenges.

In earlier times, when all diplomatic establishments were small and foreign interests less far ranging, the diplomat had no such responsibility. By and large even the most senior diplomat was a manager only in the sense that he managed his own time.

What has brought about the change, of course, is the entry of nearly every element of government into the foreign affairs field. In contrast with earlier times, the modern diplomat now finds that emanating from across the entire spectrum of government—not just from each executive department or ministry, but from almost each of their subdivisions—is an extraordinary range of foreign interests and, in a great many instances, foreign activities as well. He deals now not with but one department but with a "foreign affairs community" made up of all the elements within his government with foreign activities or interests. And these interests and activities fall in chaotic disarray on the embassies abroad, presenting for ambassadors and their staffs (and for state departments and foreign offices back home) a management problem of the first order.

The problem will not go away. Given the ever increasing dimensions of interdependence in the world, this interest and involvement of other elements of government is by no means a passing phenomenon. And as the situation will not change, the diplomat must change. A key new dimension has been added to his job.

§

Unlike many other walks of life, including governmental life, the diplomat's work in his early years tends to provide him with very little real management experience. Young officers elsewhere in government service, including in the military (and in such closely associated sister agencies in the foreign affairs community as those running information, cultural, and aid programs abroad), become managers almost from the start of their careers. But the young diplomat, especially the diplomat who has specialized in political work, tends to miss out on comparable experience because of the personal and individualistic character of his work.

The result is that many diplomats in the modern era have suddenly found themselves in important managerial positions—ambassadors, deputy chiefs of missions, or heads of large embassy sections—with almost no previous managerial experience to fall back on, save for having managed their own secretary. And here, if the truth were known, it is likely that she managed them.

Under the circumstances, many diplomats have done surprisingly well simply by relying on intelligence and the modicum of managerial experience they have been able to pick up through running a small consulate or from work on country desks and the like. But what is clearly needed is more systematic help to each diplomat in terms of management preparation. What is also needed, on the part of each diplomat, is a constant awareness as he moves up the ladder that this responsibility waits, inevitably, for those who reach the key positions of their profession. It means that the mastery of this capability must be sought with the same zeal previously reserved for the more traditional core skills.

What is also needed is a change in certain classic attitudes. It may still be fashionable to confuse management with the work of administrative officers, and look down on both; but it is not wise. The saying that "administrative officers are our valets, and now they are trying to wear our pants" (and mentally lumping together all administration and all management problems) is good only for a comfortingly snide chuckle, and a continuing misunderstanding of the real world of diplomacy. "The administrators are taking over!" is the addled cry of the hopelessly out-of-date.

To begin with, in the narrower administrative sense, being an accomplished administrative officer in today's complicated diplomatic establishments is a notable professional achievement in its own right, one fully meriting the admiration and gratitude of fellow professionals elsewhere in those establishments. Without them, their more "substantive" colleagues would be in a bad fix indeed. And, from the point of view of management skills, there is much that everyone else in the embassy can learn from them.

Management is a broader term, and a broader concept, than

administration. The diplomat who has risen to a leadership role, either in his parent organization at home or in an embassy abroad, can leave administration to the specialists who have specific experience, aptitude, and interests he does not have, but he cannot similarly put aside his broader management responsibilities. On the contrary, if he cannot properly orchestrate the complex and myriad activities of the organization which he leads, that organization simply cannot function effectively. An embassy's talents and energies will at best be only partially deployed. And the fault which cripples the work of so many embassies of so many nations, namely, the application of about 80 per cent of their effort to about 20 per cent of their target, will continue as one of diplomacy's classic problems.

Being a manager in diplomacy means having the ability to avoid just this type of thing. It requires a capability to identify targets clearly, to keep priorities always in mind, to unleash the full impact of the diverse resources available in his organization, and to apply these resources to his objectives in commensurate proportion to their objectives.

It is a capability which the diplomat can hone by carefully observing the performance of others about him—for example, the military, aid officials, information officers, all of whose work brings more management responsibility than he has had in the early and middle years of his career. It can be developed by an enlightened exchange program for younger officers, conducted by his parent organization, to offer actual assignments in these more management-oriented areas of the foreign affairs community. It can be aided by a strong element of management principles and techniques being implanted in the training courses he encounters in his early and middle years. It can be aided by senior diplomats' feeling the same responsibility to pass on what they have learned in this area as they feel with respect to the other core skills.

Because the development of this key skill is not as often aided by "opportunities for doing" as in the case of the other core skills, much will depend on the younger diplomat himself. He must seize every opportunity along the way, no matter how meager, to think and learn about this skill, a skill which because of the nature of his other responsibilities tends to be the most difficult of all to master.

For their part, the leaders of diplomatic establishments have an obligation to identify young officers with management potential and to make a special effort to expose them to assignments and training which will strengthen that potential. And, equally important, they must ruthlessly resist the traditional belief that the natural and ultimate reward of all brilliant diplomats is an assignment as chief-of mission.

A brilliant officer, if he is not also a good manager, is simply not qualified to meet the orchestration responsibilities of a modern chief of mission. A less brilliant officer, with a competent mastery of the other core skills and with a sound managerial ability, will be a far wiser choice.

There are still many key places for the brilliant nonmanager to perform, a number of which (e.g., head of a political section in a large embassy, a key member of an important negotiating team, a key position on his headquarters' policy planning council) can be more important than positions as chiefs of certain smaller missions. Valuable as their contributions can be, however, the dictates of modern diplomacy require that they be made from positions other than chief of mission.

§

The responsibility of the modern diplomat does not end with his becoming a competent manager. In addition, he must have an enduring commitment to the development of modern managerial tools and techniques for his profession and to the search for the solutions to the serious management problems which beset it.

He cannot leave this task to the management "experts," for if he does not share their efforts, they will not be expert in diplomacy's real requirements. And if he is not prepared to benefit from this work (eschewing such oft repeated and accurate but irrelevant comments as "a diplomat can never be replaced by a computer"), he will inevitably find his capabilities overwhelmed by the ever increasing diversity of his own nation's interests and efforts abroad, and the ever increasing complexities of the foreign problems with which he must deal.

Presidents and prime ministers continue to look to their diplomatic establishment as their principal staff arm in forging a national policy out of the much expanded spectrum of diverse, specialized, and often parochial foreign affairs interests throughout their governments.

They continue to expect these institutions to ensure that the government's wide-ranging activities abroad are carried out in a coordinated way, and in a manner consistent with the overall policies which have been determined.

Talent, hard work, and the mastery of diplomacy's more traditional skills have taken the diplomat, some time ago, as far as they are going to in helping him to meet his expanded responsibilities. Despite a number of brilliant individual performances along the way, the job does not get done through reliance on the older skills and by meeting the new dimensions of the job simply by "trying harder."

He must focus on the management area for help. Otherwise, first-rate people will continue to try to operate in third-rate systems, a condition which now cripples the work of so many diplomatic institutions around the world. Rather than mastering his job, he will be increasingly overrun by it. His impact will diminish, and coordination of his nation's efforts abroad will suffer.

Problems of interdepartmental anarchy in the foreign affairs area within his own government will grow, as will the related tendency of other departments of government to set up their own "in house" foreign offices and establish their own foreign services. The problem of imbalances and distortions of resources as applied to objectives will also grow. And in the end mounting presidential or prime ministerial frustration over the inability of their diplomats to get the job done will lead to their decreasing reliance upon them, and to their turning elsewhere for help.

But there is no other satisfactory place to turn. The job cannot be fragmented and parceled out to other departments and agencies. This is the last way to get a coordinated effort. Nor can it be handed over to any one of these existing organizations, because each has a specialized interest or bias.

Nor can it be handed over to presidential staffs, for example to the one which operates the nation's National Security Council machinery. Although N.S.C. staffs have both coordinating responsibility and experience, they cannot, with their relatively small size, take on the massive portions of the coordinating work which falls to the diplomatic establishments. The two are not designed to be bureaucratic rivals, but integral parts of the same system.

National Security Council machinery simply will not work if an effectively functioning diplomatic establishment is not carrying a major share of the load. In the case of the United States, if the job were turned over to an N.S.C. staff, the latter would soon have to be expanded so as to be in effect a re-creation of the State Department under a different name. It would still have the same management problems that come with bigness and complexity. It could not recruit, in any large numbers, personnel more talented or experienced than those already in the U.S. diplomatic establishment. And with the N.S.C. staff so large, a new, small staff would likely have to be created and added to the President's immediate entourage to play the role of the old N.S.C. staff. Where two organizations existed before, there could now well be three. For the remnants of the old State Department diplomatic organization would probably still exist, relegated to much reduced responsibilities primarily of a technical and housekeeping nature abroad.

An alternative institution, also in the immediate environs of the President, is his governmentwide budget office. This organization has considerable experience in, and responsibility for, the coordination of government activities. Moreover, it is accustomed to controlling the allocation of resources, one of the most valuable of all tools in any coordinating effort. Here knowledge and experience in foreign affairs are minimal, and if the job came by default to this organization, it would soon have to expand enormously. Again, in effect, it would have to re-create the State Department under its own roof.

What all this means is that if the State Department and foreign offices did not exist, something like them would have to be invented. And these new institutions, while having to deal with much the same management challenges and difficulties, would not for many years be able to assemble an array of talent and experience to match what already exists in the present diplomatic establishments. Put another way, if a fine automobile does not work because of a faulty carburetor, it makes no sense to go out and duplicate the car. You fix the carburetor.

What it also means is that the national interests, and not simply bruised diplomatic ego, are at stake in the diplomat's effort to reduce the management lags which inhibit his performance. It means that as a professional, he has an obligation to be as interested and expert in this aspect of his work as in any other.

§

It does not mean that he should be surprised or dismayed that the lag itself exists. In an era of change, many large institutions face similar gaps in their performance, and, of course, no institution, diplomatic or otherwise, is going to catch up completely, no matter how active and modern are its efforts to do so. Modernization is by definition a process which is never done. What it does mean is that he should understand how the gap has emerged and what are its key components which must be constantly worked on.

In the case of the United States, the gap, in a serious form, began to develop in the era following World War II. This was a time when diplomats around the world had little trouble in adjusting intellectually to the changed conditions of that world, but they had, and many have had ever since, great difficulty in facing up to the organizational and management requirements inherent in the new circumstances in which they now must operate.

In a time of change, they were impressively resistant to change. They were comfortable with policy making, with promoting that policy abroad, and with the other traditional roles and skills of their profession. But they remained intuitive in nature, weak in planning, and disinterested in managerial systems and techniques. They were unwilling to give the necessary priorities to training and research or to vitally important programs of exchange of personnel with other departments and agencies, now operating as important partners in the foreign affairs field. In fact, they allowed the legend to grow that assignments in any of these areas did not go to those in highest esteem, and were not the route to early promotions. Each of these attributes was, of course, a serious liability in facing the challenges of the modern era.

As brand-new agencies appeared on the scene—rich and powerful new agencies operating in the intelligence, aid, and information areas and destined to play important roles—diplomats tended to make two additional critical errors.

The first stemmed from an instinctive desire to protect the high standards and exclusiveness of their profession. They did not want the high quality of the diplomatic service invaded and watered down. And they had reason to be concerned on this score, at a time when these new agencies were being built with a rapidity which precluded uniform adherence to optimum personnel standards.

It was overly harsh for the diplomats to look on these new organizations as made up of but a few very able leaders, plus many middle-aged quasi failures whom they had recruited, and with whom they had once been to school. But it was certainly true that the personnel standards of these agencies were far from the levels they were to become.

The result was that the U.S. diplomatic establishment resisted the type of intimacy with these new organizations in the foreign affairs community, which logic now clearly suggests they should have intensely cultivated from the beginning. They protected their exclusiveness, but in the process they lost control of much of the action.

The second reaction was equally damaging. Faced with this widespread invasion of the international scene by so many government institutions, new and old, many diplomatic establishments tended to develop the rather comforting formula that while others might conduct operations and programs in the foreign affairs field, it was the diplomatic establishment which dealt with policy. Although as a theoretical distinction this may have a certain logic, as a practical matter it simply won't work. The two cannot be divorced, and any institution that wishes to have a major say in policy must have a major hand in the conduct of operations and programs. Otherwise, policy makers are talking to themselves, and the real control of policy, as it translates into action, is elsewhere.

Ironically, one of the lessons of the immediate post-World War II era is that neglect of management-lag problems tends to be greater during the eras of strong secretaries of state. The danger, of course, is that those career officials who man diplomatic establishments tend to get the preeminence and dominance of their leaders confused with their own. Their leader's position lulls them into a false sense of confidence that their own leadership role is assured, and it camouflages the need for the constantly improved management tools and machinery so essential for the maintenance of that role.

In the late 1940's and for most of the 1950's, for example, the U.S. State Department was led by two exceptionally strong secretaries, each blessed with the unswerving support of his president, and both unusually experienced, able, and dominant. No single official, however, no matter how able, can possibly dominate and coordinate anything but a small fraction of the welter of objectives and interests at loose within the government. To a remarkable degree these two men were monarchs of all they surveyed; but while what they surveyed was generally a key part, it was only a small part, of the whole. Basking in their reflected authority, professional diplomats failed during this time of major change within the U.S. foreign affairs community to keep pace with the managerial innovations which were needed to cope with a leadership and coordinating task growing more complex and difficult each year.

When a department is led by a strong secretary, morale goes up and diplomats engaged at home in intragovernmental disputes fight harder and longer, secure in the knowledge that they will be backed in the end by a strong force at the top. Both morale and aggressiveness are critically important assets for any institution, but leadership, and the effective and sensible coordination of the whole range of a nation's foreign affairs, clearly require more than a high morale and a combative stance in intramural disputes.

Narrow parochialism aside, the disputes which regularly arise within a government stem from conflicting objectives and priorities, legitimately arising in turn from a wide range of quite different intragovernment vantage points. Therefore, while strong leadership from the diplomatic establishment is essential to the effective resolution of those disputes, what is also required is managerial machinery which assures objective, systematic, and knowledgeable weighing of these conflicting interests. This machinery must be constructed in such a way that it will instill sufficient confidence among its combative participants that they will usually, if not always, be prepared to accept the conclusions reached.

Diplomats during their lifetimes will inevitably encounter a variety of styles and performances on the part of their secretaries or foreign ministers. These in turn will be much affected by the inevitably varying styles of the presidents and prime ministers they serve. Thus, while no diplomatic establishment can fail to be affected by the performance of its top leaders, it is essential that the morale and performance of its diplomats have a base and vitality of their own. A base and vitality, that is, which are independent of the almost inevitably uneven performance of their secretaries or ministers.

These separate wellsprings of a diplomat's morale and performance must flow from a dual source. First and foremost, they must stem from a confident and competent mastery of each of the core skills this book has examined. That is the most critical source. But of key importance, too, is the confidence which comes from knowing that managerial machinery is available to him, machinery which facilitates his leadership role in his government's foreign affairs community, and which unleashes rather than inhibits his impressive capabilities.

CHAPTER TEN

The Dimensions of Managerial Responsibility

IT IS AN EXAGGERATION, but perhaps not an altogether untenable one, to say that there are generally but two officials within a government who see exactly eye to eye on what the objectives and priorities should be with respect to any one particular foreign country. Those two are the ambassador to that country and the officer who operates his "country desk"—that is, his backstopping office—in his state department or foreign office back home.

The assumption is that an ambassador will feel it sufficiently important to his operations to have this key officer on the same wavelength with him, that if this is not the case a way will be found to get a new desk officer. These two officers usually see things almost identically, not under influence of ambassadorial pressure, but because they are both living with the same situation and, over a considerable time, their thinking has been conditioned by the same factors and circumstances.

But what of the departmental assistant secretary for whom the desk officer also works, and who is a key figure for all the ambassadors who serve in his region? He can never, or certainly almost never, see all matters exactly the same way as the embassy-country-desk team, because right next door will be another embassy-country-desk team which—dealing with a different and often a rival country and problem—will have reached quite different conclusions. It is not an allegation of localitis (although that can be part of the problem) to note that ambassadors often see interests in a very different light. But this natural result of differing vantage points means that no ambassador's advice can be treated as sovereign. Otherwise a nation will end up with as many policies as it has ambassadors.

And, of course, the differences within the government are just beginning. The assistant secretary's views regarding objectives, and particularly regarding priorities (developed after weighing the views of many embassies), will likely not be the same as many of his other senior departmental colleagues'. For example, to name just one of many, the assistant secretary charged with overall supervision of economic affairs often operates with somewhat differently ordered interests and, therefore, priorities from those of the regional assistant secretaries who take economic factors into account, but who tend to focus first on the political aspects of the problem they face. And so it goes on and on, just taking into account the differing vantage points within the State Department itself.

Once outside that departmental or foreign office, the differences become even more notable and more wide-ranging. A Secretary of Commerce in the past has taken the view that the number one effort, the number one priority, of every embassy in the world is export promotion. Thus, in country X, even though it lies, let us say, at the center of Arab-Israeli tensions during a particularly virulent phase of those tensions, the number one objective of the American embassy by this doctrine would be export promotion. Even if this position were not carried to such extremes, it is both likely and understandable that export promotion would be accorded a higher priority on the Commerce Department's list than on many others.

In any event, and returning to the example of country X, the Secretary of Defense at such a time would surely have a quite different set of priorities revolving around his strategic military concerns. The focus of the Secretary of State might be different still, for he will be concentrating on the role his country can play in the building and maintenance of an area peace.

And these are by no means the only government departments interested in country X. The Department of Agriculture will, among other quite different concerns, think of its potential as a customer or rival in the effort to promote U.S. foodstuffs, or of its role in the problem of food surpluses or shortages. The Department of Interior will be focusing, among other things, on country X's mineral situation. The Department of Health, Education, and Welfare will have its still different concerns, and so on and on, until practically the whole roll of government departments and agencies is heard from.

And while it is difficult enough to get conflicting viewpoints resolved within a government department, it is obviously even more difficult to get disputes about priorities and objectives resolved between departments.

In the United States, the President, of course, has the power to do this. Where the disputes become especially critical, this is often the only place that they can be resolved. He will have National Security Council or other interdepartmental machinery established for this purpose; and in the end, if the disputes are carried to his level, he can decide which of the contested objectives he approves, and in what order of priority, and what resources each department will put into the overall effort.

The President can do this, and the argument in that particular instance will be resolved. There are not sufficient hours in the day, however, for him to deal personally with any but a few of the most critical disputes which continually arise.

His Secretary of State can play a similar role, where he has the adequate backing of his President. But even when such backing is available, the Secretary can again deal with only a small portion of the myriad conflicts which arise. The President's national security inter-agency-coordinating machinery, acting in the name of the President but without his direct personal involvement, can also broker out, and, in eras when it is strong enough, actually decide disputes between warring governmental viewpoints.

But all these devices can at best deal with only a portion of the conflicts of viewpoints ranging across the spectrum of govermental departments and agencies with interests and activities abroad.

The large spillover of still unresolved conflicts into the intra-governmental community results in many of its elements' doggedly pursuing their own diverse and often parochial priorities. This results in turn in a sort of anarchy, and an uncoordinated effort abroad that at best runs off in too many directions, and at worst is working at actual cross purposes.

This anarchy is often compounded by the desire of many

governmental departments to set up their own foreign offices at home and their own foreign services abroad. This phenomenon stems of course from a strongly held conviction within these departments that their interests are not adequately represented by any department other than their own. Thus, secretaries of agriculture or commerce and their departmental colleagues are reluctant to entrust the country's agricultural or business interests abroad to the State Department, believing that it will not have the necessary knowledge or interest in the job to get it done properly, and in conflicting priority situations that state departments and foreign offices cannot be counted on to support their interests with the necessary zeal.

But while no chief of government can insist that all his other departments or ministries defer abjectly and completely to his state department or foreign ministry in all matters concerning interests abroad, neither can he permit a situation where his government, rather than having one foreign ministry, ends up operating abroad through a series of foreign offices, each representing a particular government department and a special government concern. The answer lies, of course, not in the proliferation of within-government foreign ministries, but in strengthening governmentwide confidence in the one that it already has.

As a practical matter quasi anarchy, even without the full development of sound managerial tools to cope with this problem, is generally prevented from becoming all-out anarchy for a number of reasons.

To begin with, departments or ministries will often voluntarily compromise their conflicting interests in situations where it is clear to all concerned that overriding national interests require this. In addition, there is the role of the chief of government and of his secretary of state as well as national-security-type intragovernmental machinery already referred to.

Equally important is the fact that, even where a nation's state department or foreign ministry seems to be challenged by rival foreign offices within its own government, it is the official foreign ministry which sits at the center of the process, and is possessed of the broader overall view, and has the most extensive professional personnel resources. Thus, while its role is no longer exclusive and sovereign, it still tends to be dominant.

Moreover, its position within its own government is strengthened immeasurably wherever the ground rule is still maintained that only the state department or foreign ministry can instruct an ambassador abroad. Other departments or ministries can send advice and guidance to certain categories of personnel assigned to embassies to do the work of particular interest to them, but it is the ambassador who is the commander in the field and all personnel in the embassy are subject to his jurisdiction. The department which commands the commander is in a strong position in relation to its rivals.

The solution to this problem lies beyond the logic of the state department's role, or the supplying of it with adequate clout to dominate intragovernmental rivals in the foreign field—important as both of these factors are. For in the end other departments of government will defer to the state department or foreign ministry only if they are convinced that considerations of critical importance to them will receive a fair and knowledgeable hearing. Confidence of this kind comes only from the establishment of a state department-managed system in which they remain important participants, and through which they see at first hand an objective professional weighing of the whole spectrum of governmentwide interests—including their own.

There is no one best way to set up such a system, and whatever system is installed must constantly be improved. One way, among several possibilities, is for the process to start with the country team at an embassy. The country team is in effect the ambassador's cabinet and is made up of all the section chiefs in the embassy and all the senior representatives of other government departments who also have personnel assigned to the embassy community. This group, under the ambassador's leadership, can put out on the table for careful scrutiny every possible interest and objective as seen from the vantage points of their respective organizations back home. Then, after an exhaustive search for alternatives, and after considerable discussion and evaluation among themselves, they can decide which of the possible interests and objectives should be pursued in what order of priority. Concurrently they can determine what each element of the embassy community should put behind each of these interests by way of its own resources in order that the overall apportionment of embassy time and effort will be commensurate with the relative priorities of its objectives.

The next step, in any process originating in this way in the field, is for its conclusions to be referred back home for further interdepartmental review at the assistant secretary level. Here, under the leadership of the appropriate regional assistant secretary of state, but with assistant secretaries participating from each of the other departments in government with activities or interests in the country concerned, alternatives can be reanalyzed, new alternatives can be considered, and the objectives and priorities arrived at by the country team can be reexamined, and possibly altered, in the light of headquarters' perspectives.

A committee at this level should be able to arrive at what are in effect a governmentwide set of priorities and objectives. In instances where agreement is not reached, disputes can be referred for resolution to similar interdepartmental committees at the undersecretary or deputy secretary level. In this way, interdepartmental agreement, in effect governmentwide agreement, can be reached on what that government as a whole is seeking to accomplish with respect to the particular foreign country involved, and in what order of priority.

Such a process will be in effect, even if not formally, an integral part of the President's overall national security machinery. It should also, by carrying the bulk of the load with respect to reconciling interdepartmental differences, free that machinery for handling some of the more crucial or seemingly irreconcilable disputes.

Even where disputes are resolved and agreement reached at the assistant secretary level, the process should not stop there. The conclusions should be elevated for review to the very top deputy secretary—undersecretary level of the state department or its equivalent in other foreign offices, so this top leadership can examine the conclusion agreed upon at the assistant secretary level and make certain, again after considering alternatives, that they agree with them.

This review should ideally be staffed by the policy planning office, or some other such staff which is directly attached to the principal officers of the department, and should be chaired by one of the department's undersecretary-level officers. If the top leadership of the department is not prepared to do this, they will, as is the case in a great many foreign ministries, find themselves presiding over their institutions, but not really running them. They will be abdicating to the lower-ranking assistant secretaries. They will be reigning, not ruling.

They will deal with most countries only in specialized circumstances, that is, when it is part of a crisis they must handle or the locus of a particularly difficult dispute which is brought to their level because it cannot be resolved at a lower level. If there is not some systematic way to get before them the kind of total overview of their government's policies toward a particular country—the kind of overview which emerges from the type of policy-analysis and resource-allocation procedures just described—then the department's top management simply won't know in any significant detail what their country's policy is toward that country, let alone whether they agree with it.

It is not a process which a state department's top leadership needs to go through very often with respect to each country. Perhaps once every two or three years with some of the countries which are of less significance to it. But to do it not at all, to allow its time to be preempted by crisis management and by becoming high-level case officers for specific problems (which is what most of them become), can only mean that they have in effect allowed circumstances to maneuver them out of running the department.

The programming and resource allocation system just described is subject to almost infinite variations. The point is, however, that no state department or foreign office has an adequate system now. Many do not even have the beginnings of such a system, or any real understanding of its necessity.

Any system requires continued adaptation and experiment. Whatever system, and variations on systems, are evolved, three basic criteria must be met. All departments of government involved in foreign affairs must participate; they should be led by the nation's state department or foreign ministry; and the very top officials of these latter institutions must be active participants in these systems, using them both as a means of education for themselves and as invaluable tools for breaking out of the confines of crises and special problems to meeting their across-the-board leadership responsibilities.

§

This leads logically to another key area of managerial concern: the operations of a state department's or foreign office's top leadership. Understandably a secretary of state or the foreign minister cannot himself allocate much time for directing the internal operations of the department or office he leads. His immediate responsibilities are too "outward oriented" for that—oriented, that is, toward foreign officials, the President, the Congress, the press, and the public. Nor can anyone at the assistant secretary level "run" the department because, although these are senior officials indeed, each has a specifically limited perspective and area of responsibility.

The secretary or foreign minister must turn then to the layer of leadership between himself and the assistant secretaries: the deputy secretary, the undersecretaries and the few other top officials who join them in this layer of rank just below the secretary or minister himself. In the case of the United States, this level of leadership is known as the State Department's "7th floor" for the obvious reason that, along with the Secretary, their offices are clustered there.

But "7th floors" all over the world have a difficult time indeed in carrying out their responsibility to run, under the general direction of their secretary or foreign minister, the sprawling and complex organizations which supposedly are reporting to them. The problem is that each one of these seventh-floor officials tends to have specific responsibility in the political, economic, administrative, planning, or other fields. Each develops what are often rather sizable professional staffs around him, reporting only to him and helping him pursue his own specific interests and responsibilities.

The result is the exact opposite of a cohesive leadership operation. Instead, it is a fragmented operation, with the seventh floor not acting to manage the department as a whole, but rather with each principal breaking off a section of the department and running it as something of a separate entity. To the diplomat abroad, therefore, it sometimes seems that his headquarters' operations consist not of one state department or foreign office but of many—and none in very close step with the other.

Again, there is no one best solution. Administrative reorganizations are rarely permanent, and rarely permanently resolve problems of this kind. But the answer must lie first of all in recognition that the overall responsibility for the internal operation of the department must be specifically lodged in one official, usually the number two man. While it is generally assumed that these officials around the world have this responsibility, it is surprising how often this is not the case.

In fact, number two men often find themselves set somewhat apart from the main action of the department, especially when it is led by a strong and active number one. The latter will tend to deal directly with the "6th floor," where the assistant secretaries are, for these are officials actively handling the problems with which the secretary must deal.

The result is the number two official is often figuratively relegated to the sidelines much as is the number two quarterback on a professional football team. In both cases you have to have a top-flight man for the job. He must be able to step in at any moment and perform for the number one, but when number one is on the scene the talents of number two are underused.

A variation on this is to have the number two man, at the secretary's direction, operate as the number one official for a range of lesser matters with which the secretary does not wish to deal.

Most state departments and foreign offices around the world operate with one or the other of these arrangements and most often with a combination of both.

But often, too, the other seventh-floor officials, while junior in rank to the number two, may have their authority directly from the secretary. The secretary usually transfers, lock, stock, and barrel, all his administrative and budgetary authorities to his administrative principal on the seventh floor, who then proceeds to act as his alter ego in such matters—a delegation which often goes around, not through, the more senior deputy secretary.

In any event, the point to be made is that the first key to the solution of the seventh-floor leadership problem is that all responsibility and authority for the internal running of the department must be lodged with one man, and in most instances that official will be the one next ranking behind the secretary or foreign minister.

And the second key lies in recognizing that no one official can by himself stay on top of, and coordinate, all the activities of a ministry. This is true even of a relatively small foreign ministry, of a relatively small country. It is surely true of the larger countries' foreign departments.

State departments or foreign ministries must be run by a collegium of senior seventh-floor officials who, under the number two man's leadership, exercise the authority that the secretary has vested, not in them, but in him. They must accept cabinet-type collective responsibility for the way that the department operates. The fragmenting impact of large separate staffs attached directly to individual seventh-floor officials should be avoided. Rather, whether secretariat, policy planning, administrative and budget, or whatever, they should be regarded as common staffs working for the collegium as a whole.

It may be that as time goes on, quite different and far better systems for running a foreign office can be devised. Certainly, the one just described requires constant improvement and adjustment. But the key point is that diplomats cannot operate up to their potential in a department where the top leadership function is divided up among a number of quasi-independent chiefs—where each chief grabs off a piece of the department to run, and where these chiefs then become so bogged down in specific problems that they do not really run that piece in any event.

§

Nor is it just the problem of effective "7th-floor" leadership with which the career diplomat must concern himself. In many cases, the managerial lag on the sixth floor (at the assistant secretary level) is even greater than on the seventh floor. Assistant secretaries have deputies, but, again, these tend to be specialized and limited in their responsibilities. Regardless of what the table of organization shows, only one man in a large bureau often ends up with responsibility for considering all the problems of the bureau as a whole. And that man is the assistant secretary himself, one of the busiest of all the capital's senior officials. Everyone else will have responsibility for only a piece of the whole.

Given the breakneck pace of the assistant secretary's working day, and working evening, and the unending problems which fall constantly in his lap, he has few moments available for the thoughtful overview. Rarely can he back off and look at his region as a whole, resort his priorities, and get all his problems and objectives back in perspective. Perhaps he can turn to this when he stops for a stop light on his way home, or for some other equally fleeting moment. Often, it seems, there is no other time.

A bureau can have strong, forceful, and often brilliant figures as assistant secretaries, but any complex organization run in this way is not well run. Assistant secretaries, too, need a collegium to help them, along with a planning/devil's advocate group, and other managerial tools.

All diplomats must concern themselves with these problems. An institution that still runs itself like a country store, that cannot effectively lead itself, can hardly hope to lead the other bureaucracies involved in their government's overall efforts in the foreign field.

§

A key area of management concern must be the development of a strong policy reevaluation system, for a long time one of the most neglected areas of management interest. Inspection teams were sent regularly to the field, but these tended to inspect people and accounts, and to focus primarily on how those staffing and leading an embassy were performing. They did not inspect policy.

It often seemed that the only persons doing that were wandering congressmen, or newspapermen, or private travelers who had contributed heavily to the last political campaign and, therefore, could get the ear of someone highly placed back home to air concerns which might, or might not, be valid.

Secretaries and foreign ministers, on the other hand, tended to rely primarily on the appropriate regional assistant secretaries and ambassadors to monitor the needs for change. Although these officials are hardly oblivious either to what is going on or to the fact that changed conditions require changed policies, they are, however, not a source on which to place complete reliance for critically important reevaluation.

The reason is simple enough. Ambassadors and assistant secretaries give, in Dean Rusk's phrase, the most exhaustive "prayerful Presbyterian consideration" to what the policies in an area should be. After having carefully weighed all the factors as they have seen them, however, and after having finally, but firmly, reached their basic conclusions, their natural tendency is to pursue the policy lines they have settled upon with all the drive and persistence they can command. This is never, of course, an easy task, and understandably it, rather than the reevaluation process, tends to usurp the lion's share of assistant secretarial and ambassadorial time and energy.

In any event, prudence requires that secretaries and foreign ministers be able to turn for a reevaluation of policies to officers other than those personally committed to those policies and charged with the responsibility for carrying them out. Logic dictates that policy reevaluation can best be done, not by traveling amateurs, no matter how gifted, but by the professional diplomats themselves.

What is needed is an inspection corps of professional diplomats to inspect policy in addition to people and accounts. Policy inspections must be regarded as much the more important part of an inspector's job. Coming on the scene without responsibility for either the development or the implementation of current policies, they must answer for their chiefs back home certain fundamental questions. The first is whether the policy that headquarters thinks is being carried out in the field is in fact being carried out. Top leadership at home must have a means, independent of reliance solely on those operating the policies, to check on this. Second is whether the policies conducted still make sense, or whether they are being carried forward by the forces of momentum into an era where changed conditions have rendered them obsolete or partially obsolete. And the third responsibility is to recommend professionally sound alterations in policy where they have found that momentum has put things out of kilter.

Of course, an inspection system of this kind can never be infallible and its judgments under questions two and three may or may not be correct. But such a system, infallible or not, provides a critically important cross-checking management tool that no well-run diplomatic establishment should be without.

§

Computers and other increasingly sophisticated modern management tools and processes are also necessary for effective management.

Computers are a subject concerning which many diplomats seem determined to remain steadfastly ignorant. Yet these and other new management tools have an essential role to play in the effective functioning of any modern diplomatic effort. Granted that no computer can ever take the place of a gifted, experienced diplomat. But one of the most critically important of all elements in the diplomat's work is information, and computers offer resources in this regard that no diplomat in the past knew or even dreamed of.

I am not speaking here of the routine administrative assistance (record keeping, payrolling, keeping track of action assignments and dates when completed action is due, etc.) that computers can provide for any large administratively burdened organization, but rather of the special contribution they can make to the diplomat's substantive work.

Information is not just important to diplomacy, it is its life's blood. Thousands of words flow back to headquarters from post, day after day, year after year. Only through computers can the diplomat of the future hope to avoid being drowned by the sea of information that, inexorably and massively, accumulates each day. It is only through a well-developed computer system that he can retrieve from this mass of information all the pertinent portions which relate to whatever subject he is dealing with at the moment.

It is remarkable how often problems in diplomacy repeat themselves, or at least how often things happen which are similar to what has happened before. On such occasions, the computer should regurgitate what exactly was done before, what alternative solutions were considered, and why they were rejected. It should show whether the matter was taken to the U.N. and, if so, when and what factors were considered regarding wording of resolutions. It should show, in short, all the factors taken into account before deciding on the moves that were finally made.

Each crisis of the present need not be handled as one in the past, but it is foolishness of the first order not to have available the benefit of past experience in dealing with the present. With computers, this can be done systematically and thoroughly by the pressing of buttons—a far superior device to the rather hit-or-miss methods of the past: searching through dingy file drawers, and trying to find someone working down the hall who happened to have been involved in the earlier crisis, and whose memory for events of long ago remains more or less reliable.

As previously noted, to develop an effective computer system for a diplomatic service requires computer technicians, on the one hand, and practicing diplomats who understand what computers can and cannot do, on the other. If effective and essential computer support is to be instituted for diplomatic services, and then made constantly more sophisticated and useful, professional diplomats as a whole must be willing to learn much more about the computer sciences than they have been as these lines are written.

The same can be said for a number of other areas. Take, for another example, the field of quantitative analysis. Diplomats spend their lives analyzing and predicting, yet their knowledge of the extent to which this important field can and cannot help them is practically nonexistent. Here again, diplomats of the future must seek a knowledge even the need for which is now scarcely understood.

There are innumerable additional areas of managerial responsibility where diplomats should sustain an enlightened concern. How can a diplomatic establishment learn to think ahead—well beyond, that is, the two to four years that often at most can now be managed? What are the best devices for guarding against that insularity which plagues so many diplomatic institutions, and which is so fatal to their creative powers? What percentage of a diplomat's career should be spent in training, and in what areas should this training be focused? What proportion of a diplomatic establishment's resources should be diverted to research? What percentage of that research can be effectively and economically farmed out to the academic or other nongovernmental research communities? What should be the size and nature of its own research organization? What percentage of that organization should be manned by permanent research specialists and what percentage by regular career diplomats on rotating assignments? These and many similar management problems have simply not been sufficiently thought through by the corps of professional diplomats for whose support these services and activities were created in the first place.

CHAPTER ELEVEN
Personnel Policy

PERSONNEL POLICY IS A SUBJECT diplomats traditionally like to complain about, and dislike to learn about.

It is a luxury they can no longer afford. Today, the ability of any diplomatic service to perform depends almost entirely on the quality of the personnel policies which both shape and support it. It is a subject, therefore, in which the modern diplomat must take a deep and career-long interest. Unfortunately, as he passes beyond the complaining stage and begins to immerse himself in the problems involved, he soon finds this to be one of the most difficult of all areas in which to effect sound and proper solutions.

There is, for example, the increasingly difficult problem of balancing generalists versus specialists. The diplomat's instincts tend almost always to be on the side of the generalist, but, as in most other professions, the era of the specialist has arrived. Given the ever increasing specialization and complexity of modern life, this is not a trend which is likely to disappear.

In building an American football team, one cannot start out with personnel all of whom are ideally suited to play left end, and then expect success by having the next best left end play quarterback, the third best play right tackle, and so on. But that is what, in a figurative oversimplification, a great many diplomatic establishments have continued to do—long after the need for increasing specialization has become apparent.

In the United States it has been, for years, incorrectly asserted that all its diplomats came from the rich, Protestant, Anglo-Saxon, Ivy League circles of the eastern and western seaboards. It is, to use the vernacular, a "bum rap." The ethnic and geographical spread of those entering the diplomatic service has been an impressive one for some time now.

The critics should have been concerned for a different reason. For career diplomats still have a sameness of background which, in a sense, is as marked today as it was in earlier years when they were in fact pretty much all rich and social, and from the two seaboards only. Rich or poor, black or white, from the Ivy League or the newest and most obscure of colleges, scratch beneath a young diplomat's skin today and you will almost always find a liberal arts, history, or political science major, or a background closely similar. It is, of course, a valuable background and likely to continue to be the one most often needed. But obviously if an institution is to succeed in this day and age, it must have within its resources a range of aptitudes and backgrounds. It cannot get the job done by relying only on "left ends" no matter how brilliant and able they may be.

There remain the very difficult problems of how specialized a diplomatic service should become, and in what areas. What exact range of aptitudes should a diplomatic institution set out to recruit, and in what relative numbers? How many political officers are required? How many economic? To what degree is it wise to have these officers further specialized along geographic lines? And what is really meant by political and economic specialists, when both need to have a good deal of background in the other's area? What percentage of a diplomatic service's personnel should be administrative support specialists, and at what levels in the rank structure?

How many of the more specialized specialists will be needed? In the years ahead, for example, international scientific matters involving environment, satellite communications, and a growing host of other matters are certain to play an increasingly critical role in the relations between states. All diplomats will obviously need a better scientific background than they have needed heretofore. But how many physicists and other pure scientists must be recruited, and what percentage of these can be consultants, and what percentage should be full-time career-long colleagues? And which specific categories in the pure sciences are needed, and how often will the M.A. degree rather than the Ph.D. suffice?

How many modern weapons experts must be on hand, or how many agricultural experts—to name but two categories necessary to deal on an even footing with those departments playing an ever more important foreign relations role? How many doctors or other key support specialists does a modern diplomatic service need? How many communicators to man the code rooms, how many nurses and for which embassy communities, how many security officers, and so on and on?

Should consular work be a separate specialization of its own, to take another example? An officer doing pure consular work obviously needs some political and economic background, but basically his talent must be a bureaucratic one. "Bureaucratic" in the best sense of that term, in that he enjoys each day dealing with a great many people, making myriad decisions and moving much essential paperwork accurately and expeditiously. In many ways, the ideal officer for this work is the same type that the domestic departments of government are recruiting as management interns, not the type of person generally sought out by diplomatic establishments.

Almost everyone agrees that it would be a mistake to have so many consular specialists on hand within a diplomatic service that it precludes its other diplomatic personnel, especially its younger personnel, from getting consular experience. The phrase "almost everyone" has to be employed because there are always a few young diplomats who echo the age-old complaints against being relegated to "stamping visas" for foreigners and performing "hand-holding" protection and welfare services for traveling fellow citizens.

But in retrospect they realize, or they should realize, that consular work involves not only valuable managerial experience but also, and even more important, dealing hour after hour with people. It means dealing with the good and the bad, the naïve and the crafty. Through the decisions he makes, and through the other responsibilities he must carry, he becomes daily involved in their hopes and their tragedies. A diplomat, if he is to lay any real claim to that title, must be able to handle people well. There is no place where he can learn more about that than in a consulate.

He must learn, too, when to say no. And how to say no under pressure. And how to say it with both firmness and grace. For a diplomat this is a capability every bit as important as it is for a pretty girl. Again there is no better place to learn it than in the cauldron of pressures brought to bear on a consulate.

The problem of staffing consulates is further complicated by the fact that most consulates and consulates general, in addition to carrying out normal consular activities, function as important branch offices of the embassy to which they report, and in this sense carry on similar functions and responsibilities. Thus, the consul general or the principal officer in a consulate must be sufficiently broad-gauged to handle these added dimensions to the consular job. In part because of this, and in part because top jobs in the more important consulates general have tended to be used as consolation prizes for political and economic officers who have not been made ambassadors, consular specialists often see the top jobs in their specialty year after year go to someone else. It is a procedure hardly conducive to building strong morale among those in the service specializing in consular work.

If it is continued, the political, economic, and other nonconsular officers must sooner or later face up to the need to man all the consular jobs in their country's diplomatic service, not just a few at the junior and middle levels for experience and more at the top for pleasure. This is something that many diplomats are reluctant to do because it would mean that a much greater percentage of their career would have to be spent in consular work than they would generally like or is the case today. But they cannot have it both ways. Either the consular specialization is abandoned and the rest of the service is prepared to staff all consular positions from top to bottom, or the consular specialization is maintained and its more gifted members are supplied in the course of their careers with sufficient broadening experience that the bulk of the top consuls and consuls general jobs can be manned by those specializing in this work. A special consular corps cannot be effectively maintained if the bulk of its members are relegated only to its lesser jobs.

Building a strong consular service is an objective many diplomatic establishments around the world recognize in theory but neglect in practice. It is a serious mistake. Consular officers come into far more frequent contact with host-country citizens than do any of their colleagues elsewhere in the embassy. For this reason alone it is obviously essential that this important effort be carried out in a highly effective and creditable way. It is their consular colleagues, too, who each day meet, and have the opportunity to assist, far more of their own fellow citizens than are ever in touch with other elements of an embassy. Whether a diplomatic service makes a good or a poor impression on its fellow citizens is directly influenced in large measure by the caliber of its consular performance.

In turn, the question of whether a diplomatic service can build a "constituency" of supportive customers is much affected by the work of these officials. As is so often pointed out, most other departments of government have far greater opportunities through their service functions to build constituencies in the body politic of their own country than do diplomatic establishments, and this has an important bearing in terms of public and congressional budgeting and other matters. Consular services, and a few other activities such as those of the passport office, represent what limited opportunities diplomatic establishments have to build constituent support, and they should make the most of them.

The desire to build constituent support, however, should not preclude a constant reevaluation of the appropriate uses of the services being rendered. All consular officers of all nations have had to deal with far more travelers from their own lands than was the case when most of these services orginated. In sheer numbers they also find themselves dealing with far more foreign visa applicants and matters of this kind than in the past. As the number of consular officials generally does not increase in proportion to this increased work load, it is important constantly to set aside services that are no longer needed.

To make this point with an obvious example, the need for a consular officer to help an American citizen in London should be very limited. Here the traveler should be able to get along about as easily as he could, say, in Boston. On the other hand, an American traveler to a remote Asian or African country where a language barrier exists, and where the whole environment of life is very different from the American pattern, will legitimately need more assistance. As the world gets smaller, travelers even to the most faraway lands should need less and less consular support of a personal, individual nature. As this process goes on, consular officers should ever be on the lookout for the moment when they can appropriately shift their concentration to export promotion and to other supporting efforts connected to their nation's economic interests.

To return to the question of how much specialization there should be within a modern diplomatic service, about all that can be safely said is that far more specialization will be needed in the future than in the past. Specialization, like anything else, can be overdone and become so rigid that it ends up a liability rather than an asset. Without adequate specialization, however, a diplomatic institution will not be able to keep pace in the modern world. Unfortunately, there is no fixed solution to the problem. On the contrary, the relative need for various specialists will undoubtedly shift through the years as differing international problems take on shifting emphasis from one era to the next.

And what of the generalist? Is there no place in the future for this commodity upon which in the past diplomacy has placed such a value? The answer is that the concept of a generalist is still important in diplomacy, but in a somewhat redefined way. Quite apart from the fact that some of the modern specializations—for example, either the political specialists or the economic specialists—are still of a rather generalized character, *all* diplomats, regardless of their specializations, must master the same generalized qualities and skills discussed in earlier chapters.

It is these which bind the professionals together and place a common stamp on all diplomats, regardless of specialization. And when you analyze what old-time diplomats meant by the generalists, what they really meant were persons who had mastered these fundamental qualities and skills of their profession—and in this sense, the generalists remain as important in diplomacy today as they ever were.

§

Many other, closely related, managerial problems concerning personnel require all diplomats' continuing attention.

For example, there is the question of recruitment—that is, what range of aptitudes should be brought into the service each year and in what relative numbers? It is difficult enough to get a sound fix on the needs of the present, and for many foreign offices, the problem of ascertaining future needs is so difficult that, in effect, they make no real effort to do so. Instead, they keep on recruiting for the future as if future needs will be identical with those of the present, a procedure almost guaranteed to produce serious future imbalances. It is not just that there will be shortages in key specialized areas. Surpluses of personnel in various other categories can be an almost equal problem.

What is needed are annually amended projections of future personnel needs which, in turn, control the recruiting process. While this is far easier said than done, and can only be done infallibly if one has powers of infallible prophecy, it is a task which must receive a far more sophisticated effort in the future than it has generally had in the past.

§

Effective promotion systems and soundly designed efficiency reports are other criteria of effective management. And along with these comes the question of where to balance out the need for constantly pruning the less effective performers from a diplomatic service with the need for a reasonable degree of job security. If a pruning process of any serious kind is to be maintained, what are the most effective and desirable—and not just the minimum—safeguards and standards of fairness required to make it credible and acceptable?

Certain fundamental principles must be built into each of these processes. First and by no means the least is the obligation that every rating officer has to build the strongest possible diplomatic service for his country, which means that throughout his career he must have the courage to write candid personnel ratings frankly calling attention to all consequential weaknesses of the officer rated. This is not a type of courage uniformly found among rating officers, and of all the types of courage there are, this is perhaps the least pleasant.

Of equal importance is the principle that all factors to be rated must be explicitly understood by the officer to be rated before the rating period begins. They must never be developed and presented to him only after the rating period is completed and the rating is prepared.

All rated officers should see everything that is written concerning them, and then have the opportunity to make written comments of their own for inclusion in the same report. Where rated officers

believe that the report written on them is so unwarranted or uninformed, or in any other way is so unfair and prejudicial, that it should
be removed altogether from the report, there must be competent and
independent procedures available to review and adjudicate this.

Promotion panels must then base their judgments only and
completely on the written record—that is, on efficiency reports the
contents of which, as just noted, are fully known to the rated officer.

Officers designated by whatever process for "selection out" of the
service must have an appellate process available through which the
fully revealed grounds for the decision can be challenged and the
matter reviewed again by officials independent of the initial
procedures.

Great care must be taken not to make those procedures so
cumbersome that they fall of their own weight. Similarly, ways must
be found to ensure that rating officers will not undermine these
procedures by filing bland reports which, because they do not offend,
carry no risk that their author will become entangled in the burdens of
defending unpopular appraisals before appellate panels. If too many
written reports become too bland, then the promotion process consciously or unconsciously will begin to turn at least in part to oral
grapevine appraisals. And any system which operates, even in part, on
such a basis inevitably builds into itself the very evils, and more, that
all sound rating and promotion procedures are designed to avoid.

Experience has shown that of all managerial challenges faced by
diplomatic establishments, the development of sound rating, promotion, and pruning procedures is among the most intractable. Each
wave of personnel officials, after an agonized weighing of all the
factors involved, tends to arrive finally at firmly held views
regarding the most desirable solutions for each of these problems.
And so do their successors. Because of the obvious difficulty of this
subject, however, and the inevitable dissatisfaction with whatever
solutions are currently in vogue, the successors will almost always
disagree with the solutions arrived at by their predecessors.

The wit of man has generally been able to devise only a limited
range of alternative solutions for each of these problem areas. Dissatisfaction with one set of remedies leads almost inevitably to a return to
what was tried before, or to some rather slight variant of it. This
results in a sort of pendulum process in personnel matters. This

process, this constant changing back and forth of the ground rules for advancement, is one of the most irritating and unsettling of all the problems with which most diplomats must contend.

Although the difficulties inherent in these problems preclude the elimination of the pendulum process altogether, some of its more pronounced swings can be eliminated if all diplomats will take it upon themselves not just to be experts on the shortcomings of the existing system (which all diplomats consider themselves to be), but also to become equally expert on the demerits of all available alternatives. This should slow the pressures for change for change's sake. Eventually, it may also bring, after further trial and error, a sustainable consensus on solutions which, despite defects, are on balance the best.

§

A program for the selection out of the less outstanding performers, if soundly and fairly run, can be an important asset to any diplomatic service. But selection out must not be operated so that an officer is threatened by it throughout his career. Few people do their best work with a sword of Damocles perpetually poised above their head.

Selection out should operate primarily at two points in an officer's career. The first should be relatively early on when his service has had a few years to look at him, but when he is still young enough to start over in a new career. If an officer comes over this first threshold, he should then have reasonable assurances that he has a number of years ahead of him in the diplomatic service (unless he should do something which would precipitate his dismissal "for cause"—a procedure from which no official can ever be immune). He should certainly not be guaranteed promotions during this period. He should be guaranteed against being turned out after it is too late to get effectively started on a new career, but too early to qualify for a pension.

A number of years later, when the officer has reached his fifties, there should be a second threshold of relatively severe enforced retirement. This latter would be roughly the equivalent of what happens in the military. Only a few of many valuable colonels pass on to the general ranks. An officer who leaves the service at this second threshold leaves with the satisfaction that comes with many years of responsible and interesting service, and from the knowledge that he has qualified for an immediate and respectable pension.

It can be argued, of course, that in a service which benefits from a highly competitive personnel system, its officers should not be given a free ride in their middle years, that such a procedure undercuts the very factor that distinguishes a diplomatic service from other, less competitive, government bureaucracies.

Such an argument does not stand scrutiny. Few other elements of the government have anything like the application-to-acceptance rate that characterizes most diplomatic services. In the case of the United States, for example, eight to ten thousand applicants each year take lengthy written examinations for approximately one hundred new places. With that kind of competition to begin with, and then with anywhere from five to eight subsequent years of opportunity to judge the on-the-job performance, it seems clear that the service is not taking much of a chance on those who pass over the first threshold.

There is always the possibility that someone later will run out of steam or surface serious defects incompatible with his profession, but this will be rare, and in any event a small price to pay for a more humane service. And during the middle years between the two thresholds, promotions should still be on a competitive basis—it is only tenure which should be guaranteed. In fact, even with a threshold system, or some variant of it, the danger still is likely to be that the service is too competitive, rather than not competitive enough. Fortunately, as noted earlier, diplomatic services have considerable room at the top. Their organizational structures do not have to look like a triangle, ever narrowing in its higher reaches. Rather they should generally resemble the shape of a pear. The base is smaller than the middle; and past the middle there is a gradual, but not sharp, tapering to the top; and the very top itself (in the form of a number of senior ambassadorships) still has considerable width to it.

Even so, however, most services manage to retain more senior officers than they need, and nothing is more deadening to the service than to have many more high-ranking officials on active duty than there are jobs for. The spectacle of these senior and successful diplomats unemployed and "walking the corridor" is bad enough. The alternative, adopted by many services, of putting these officials to work in lesser jobs, and thus denying these to younger officers who should be gaining experience in them, is even worse in terms of the long-term health of service.

Thus, a major management problem for any diplomatic service is this: when should effective and successful officers who have passed the second threshold and have performed with distinction in the top echelons of the service be asked to leave? The question arises not because there are more of them than there are senior jobs, and not because their usefulness is now diminished in any way by age, but because any career system must continually and inexorably make room at the top so younger members can move upward at a measured but appropriate pace.

On any given day the most important immediate assets of a diplomatic service are its most experienced operatives. In a dangerous world, it always seems unwise to put them aside. But just as military services must retire general officers who are by no means over the hill to avoid promotion stagnation in the lower ranks, so must diplomatic services continually retire competence and experience at the senior ranks to make room for younger officers coming up. This is not a "youth must be served" principle. Rather it is the heavy but inevitable price that must be paid for the maintenance of a healthy and vital service.

§

Another important area of managerial responsibility, and one almost uniformly neglected in the past, is the appropriate utilization of women. "One cannot deny," observed a diplomatic writer of long ago, "but that it hardly accorded with the dignity of a king to be represented by women." Outmoded as this concept is, too many foreign offices apparently still fail to recognize that approximately half of the brainpower in the world is lodged in female heads, and that it makes no sense whatsoever to attempt to deal with the critical problems facing world diplomacy by drawing on only half of the world's available brainpower.

The traditional rebuttal to this has been that women have other roles and responsibilities in society which preclude their participating in the areas so long dominated by the male half of the population.

This is a rationalization which in the modern era will simply not bear examination. For example, diplomatic services employ women in large numbers for secretarial duties, and these duties require just as long a working day as that of the officers for whom they work. The assumption apparently is that women, because of family responsibilities, should not be officers in a diplomatic service but it is quite all right for them, in very large numbers, to occupy the more subordinate roles, despite the fact that these entail every bit as prolonged absences from their families each day as do officer positions. It is a double standard which will not bear scrutiny. It is not only unfair, it is stupid.

Another absurdity is the traditional rule that the relatively few women in a diplomatic service must resign if they marry, even if they marry other diplomats. At the foreign office back home, where most diplomats spend one third to one half of their career, there is always room for both to remain in active-duty positions, and most diplomatic services have a range of assignments abroad that present very little difficulty in finding a post where both a husband and wife can serve.

When husband-and-wife officer teams were first installed in the U.S. diplomatic service, considerable opposition surfaced, arguing that a wife who has worked all day is not going to be as fresh and as helpful to her husband as a nonworking wife in the conduct of his evening representational responsibilities. This is a proposition subject to challenge, but even if true it is a small price to pay for a system which can so markedly broaden diplomacy's brainpower base.

What if a woman diplomat marries not another diplomat but a painter or author or some other husband whose work is not tied to a specific locality? There is, of course, no reason whatsoever why the traditional foreign service roles cannot be reversed, with the husband accompanying the wife around the world as a dependent, instead of vice versa.

Simple proximity will tend to result in a fair share of diplomats marrying one another, and proximity again will result in a percentage of women diplomats marrying lawyers or businessmen or others whose jobs are located in the capital city when these diplomats spend their tours at home in their foreign offices. This again presents an important opportunity to retain female brains in diplomatic estab lishments. If her husband cannot travel as either a fellow diplomat or a dependent, then the state department or foreign office should have a sufficiently flexible assignment policy that from then on that particular female official should have all her assignments at headquarters.

There will be some instances when marriage will preclude the continuation of a diplomatic career. If a female officer marries a husband who cannot travel and whose locus is fixed outside of the capital city, then they must obviously make a choice between his job and hers. And in any marriage, if there are children, the wife will have to put aside her career for a period to have these children and perhaps to be with them for a time when a mother's presence seems the most necessary. The central point is that the locus problem is avoided in a surprising number of distaff diplomatic marriages, and the crucial periods when a mother's responsibilities to her children completely preempt her time tend to be a relatively small percentage of her total lifetime.

§

If diplomatic establishments must guard against majority discrimination, i.e., against women, they have an equal obligation to eliminate discrimination against racial or other minorities. Again, the reason for this does not rest alone on considerations of justice, important as these considerations are. Minorities, too, have their proportionate share of their nation's brainpower. Any national diplomatic establishment which shuts itself off consciously or unconsciously from its fair share of these brains is, again, simply crippling its ultimate potential.

There is still another important source of brainpower that diplomatic services unconsciously, but again almost uniformly, shut themselves off from. These are the people who work for them in relatively menial—certainly far below officer level—positions; not because they are not just as bright and potentially just as able as the officers whom they serve, but because they have never had the opportunity to get the university education which has become the entrance ticket to so many professions.

Of course, through a combination of luck and persistence there are some in every walk of life who overcome this handicap. When I was first an assistant secretary, I had a friend, also a State Department assistant secretary, who not too many years earlier had started his government career with a high school education and a job as a clerk in the Treasury Department. He had risen to this senior office (in which he performed with much distinction) through both his own great ability and the enlightened support of the many supervisors he encountered along the way. But the element of chance had played its part, and years later when I was responsible for State Department administration, I used to visit the huge offices filled with clerical and even more junior employees and, looking out over the sea of faces, wonder how many of the persons there had the same great potential as my friend—a potential which had never surfaced because of circumstances of their lives over which they had no control.

In any event, sound management of any diplomatic establishment requires a systematic combing over of this resource as well. This can be done through the establishment of a "mustang" program, patterned after the military service, whereby each year a number of nonofficer personnel are moved up to officer status—personnel who through subsequent training and opportunity are enabled to perform up to a potential which would otherwise be lost. In fairness, the managers owe such a program to their subofficer employees. In self-interest, they owe it to themselves.

§

Most foreign offices should also do better, on grounds of both fairness and self-interest, in the management of the careers of their secretarial staff. In our modern era diplomatic establishments cannot, quite literally, run without them. The performance of any officer, from the most junior to secretary of state or foreign minister, is affected positively or negatively by the competence of his secretary. In fact, the secretaries to the more senior officials in any diplomatic establishment occupy positions of an importance which often exceeds that of many officer positions elsewhere in the organization.

There was, not so long ago, a State Department regulation which read that anyone who had attained a certain grade or higher was to be considered an officer—except secretaries. While that could be promptly remedied, the attitude which prompted such derogatory treatment of these skilled and essential professionals is slower to change.

The job description of secretaries does not include being a maid, coffee waitress, and runner of personal errands, and if she is willing (as most secretaries are) to do any or all of these things, it should be recognized and appreciated for the gracious and voluntary act that it is. In return, she is surely entitled to something better than the traditional, thoughtless mismanagement of her time, which leaves her underemployed through much of her day and then loaded with essential work just at quitting time.

As for officer status, this should automatically be accorded when the importance of a secretarial position rests on factors beyond the mastery of basic technical secretarial skills. When the exercise of judgment and the key capacity to anticipate become central to the job, she is in effect an executive secretary doing officer work and deserving of officer pay and status.

Recently, the U.S. State Department inaugurated a "Secretary of the Year" award involving a significant tax-free cash prize for its annual recipient. Other diplomatic establishments would do well to emulate this, and all diplomatic organizations should be constantly on the lookout for ways to strengthen the esprit and effectiveness of this invaluable resource.

CHAPTER TWELVE

Human Relations within the Service

UNFORTUNATELY, FOREIGN OFFICES around the world suffer from two lags, not one. In addition to the management lag discussed in the preceding pages, almost every diplomatic institution also suffers from a serious human-relations gap, or lag, as well.

In the past, it was the nearly universal tradition to run the human-relations side of diplomatic institutions in a distinctly paternalistic way. By and large, the officials directing these organizations tried to be fair in the treatment of their personnel, and to correct injustices whenever and wherever they believed they had taken place.

In most foreign services, a sort of informal grievance system often worked reasonably effectively. The organizations were not large, and if someone believed he was receiving unfair treatment of some kind, he almost always knew someone who knew someone in authority who could look into the matter and set it right if he was satisfied of the justice of the grievant's case.

The employee had no real standing in the process. He was entirely dependent on the good will and sense of fairness of his bosses. If a senior official in authority was prepared (as he usually was) to look into the case, fine. If he was willing to give the grievant an opportunity to present his side of the story, fine. But he did not have to do this, and if a grievant received a fair and independent adjudication, this was not as a matter of right, but based entirely on the willingness of a key senior official to do the right thing as he saw it.

Diplomats found the administrative ground rules of their careers constantly shifted back and forth, often in a bewildering and unsettling way. And this was done without their having the least say in these decisions which had such an important impact on their lives and careers.

In those earlier times, the tradition was to face such circumstances with a stiff upper lip and to consider the resultant irritants, hardships, and occasional blatant injustices as necessary burdens in a career that also carried with it many balancing compensations.

This is not to suggest that nothing was done in the past to strengthen the voice of diplomats on these matters within their own parent organization. But they were not steps which, in modern times, would meet even the most minimal of acceptable standards.

For example, I recall years ago, as a very young assistant secretary in the U.S. State Department, going to one of my superiors, the then deputy under secretary for administration, to complain about a directive he had just issued to the effect that henceforth the director general of the Foreign Service was to be regarded as having assistant secretary rank. The gist of my complaint was that by adding in this way to the numbers of persons with assistant secretary rank he was cheapening the coin. The deputy under secretary, at that time one of America's most senior, gifted, and famous diplomats, responded with what now seems to me to have been remarkable restraint.

It was remarkable in that he refrained altogether from commenting on what my own recent appointment at such a tender and inexperienced age might have done to the standing of the office which I was now so zealously guarding. Instead, he carefully explained the rationale for the step he had taken. There was, he pointed out, no law or rule which required any of the other assistant secretaries or higher positions in the State Department to be occupied by career Foreign Service officers. The director general must always be a Foreign Service officer, however. Thus the step he had taken would guarantee that in the future members of the career service would always have at least one spokesman of assistant secretary rank to look after their interests.

It was a decent idea, decently motivated, but as inadequate to the standards of later times as was the informal grievance system that existed beside it.

Fortunately, the problem of closing the human relations gap in diplomatic institutions is far easier than closing the management gap.

There are, to be bluntly undiplomatic, no really modern foreign offices upon which others can pattern their progress in a managerial sense. Within many countries, however, many organizations of various kinds have faced and surmounted the problems of fair and modern human relations. Here foreign offices do not have to pioneer. They can draw heavily upon this extensive and relevant experience.

A modern human relations policy in any diplomatic organization must rest on several critically important elements.

The first of these is the existence of a management-employee relations system that will give real "clout"—that is, a very strong voice—to employees in matters of general personnel policy. Opinions will differ, and differ sharply, as to the exact shape of such a system, but the important thing is that whatever its shape and form, it has certain fundamental ingredients. The employees—that is, the members of the diplomatic service—must have the right, if they so choose, to elect an organization to be their exclusive representative in dealing with the service's senior personnel officials. Second, if diplomats do choose to be represented in this way, senior personnel officials must first discuss with the exclusive representative any changes they wish to make in personnel policy and, before its implementation, obtain the employee representative's approval. Next, and conversely, senior personnel authorities are obligated to discuss with the exclusive representative any changes the latter wishes to propose in existing policies. If, in the discussions which follow, agreement is not reached concerning the changes proposed either by personnel officials or by the employee representative, the dispute must go to an independent adjudicative unit, knowledgeable about the principles of enlightened personnel policies and the special requirements of the diplomatic profession, and empowered to make binding decisions.

Through such a system, diplomats can have a powerful voice in the development of the basic personnel policies which have such an important bearing on their careers. It is, of course, a cumbersome system for the personnel managers, compared to earlier times when their decisions faced no such inhibiting procedures. But because it builds an essential and healthy safety valve into the system, it is a small price indeed for the benefit achieved.

It does something more. While a system such as this obviously and appropriately gives employees an influence and authority they did not possess in earlier times, it burdens them with a responsibility they once put aside.

Personnel policy decisions tend to be difficult, often presenting dilemmas for which there are no completely satisfactory solutions. For years senior personnel authorities had to face these dilemmas alone, with the role of their employee-colleagues limited to the traditional one of roundly criticizing whatever solutions were finally presented.

Now these same colleagues, through their exclusive representative, must face up to the same dilemmas, and to the extent their views are accepted by personnel authorities (or, failing that, are confirmed by the adjudicative process), must share responsibility for the solutions which emerge. Under such a system, personnel authorities will be far less sovereign than once they were—but they also will be far less lonely.

When a system of this kind is first installed, it tends to suffer from the inexperience of both the employees and the personnel managers. It is not easy to replace a paternalistically run personnel system with one which is essentially far less authoritarian, and far more combative, yet still critically dependent for its success on broad areas of common understanding and common objectives. The growing-pains period when both the diplomat-employees and management's senior personnel officials are learning what it takes to make the new system work can often be a difficult one.

During this critical period—and, equally importantly, in the years that follow—two principles must be kept constantly in mind. The first is that in the heat of controversy, vigorous questioning of the validity of both the reasoning and the conclusions of others is not only fair game, it is essential to the success of the system. Questioning the character and motives is something else. That is a mucker's game, which disfigures and in the end undermines any sound employer-relations structure of this kind. And secondly, in operating such a system, both sides must remember their schooling as diplomats—and avoid nonnegotiable demands like the plague.

There remains, finally, the question of whether the organization elected to be the exclusive representative of the diplomats in their dealings with management on personnel-administration ground rules must be strictly a labor organization or whether this function can be performed by a professional organization of diplomats which has as a separate objective the constant search for ways to advance the professionalism of the service. By this is meant an organization which will, in carrying out one set of functions, act as a labor union in its dealing with management, and in carrying out its other function perform the traditional role and activities of any professional organization.

In diplomatic establishments there is no compelling reason why a professional organization cannot perform both roles, and many diplomats may prefer to belong to a hyphenated labor-professional organization which has the dual objective of improving working conditions on the one hand and upgrading professional excellence and resulting capabilities for service on the other. The diplomat should not be forced to choose this type of organization if he has decided to have an exclusive representative. If he wants a more orthodox labor organization to carry out this function, well and good. The point is, he should be free to make his own choice, and the rules should not limit him to one or the other.

§

A sound human-relations system also requires a modern grievance procedure. It is not the function of a grievance system to alter personnel policy; that is the job of the employee-management relations system. In a grievance procedure, the grievant is not trying to change personnel policy or rules of fairness currently in effect. Rather he is asserting that he has not been dealt with as existing policies and rules require. The employee-management relations system deals with collective concerns; grievance procedures are for individual complaints.

A modern grievance system requires established procedures available to a grievant as a matter of right, not based on the whim or sense of fair play of management. It must be in a position to adjudicate the issues brought to it competently, thoroughly, and in a manner completely independent of management domination. In order to do this the grievance board which presides over such a system must have an independent support staff with authority to obtain all relevant information.

The grievance board's rules of procedure must be fully set out, and these must include the right to a hearing for all grievants unless all members of the board conclude, on the basis of the record presented to them, that the complaint is totally frivolous. Provisions should be available for informal prehearing efforts at resolution of the differences between management and the grievant, a process which experience shows can be effective in many instances even after a formal grievance has been filed. The informal stage should be waivable, however, whenever the grievance board determines that resort to it would be futile.

The board should be made up of members whose appointments are acceptable to both management and the employee organization, but who, once appointed, sit in an entirely independent and judicial capacity. Such a judicial board is preferable to a tripartite board, where two of the three members are representatives of the parties concerned—one member the grievant's representative, and one the representative of management. Under the latter system, the third member is selected by the first two and is their only really independent judge. What results in effect is a board with two partisans and a third figure who does all the deciding, but who in the process often tries to broker out compromise solutions reflecting, in part at least, the views of both his warring colleagues. In a judicial board, all members act as objective judges, none as partisan representatives.

A grievance board must also have the power to give prompt and effective redress, whenever, on the basis of their deliberations, they conclude that the grievant is entitled to this.

§

A modernly run human-relations system rests on the constant search by management for ways to strengthen the elements of due process in their administrative dealings with their diplomat-employees.

The reference here is not just to improved standards for the handling of breach of security or other disciplinary activities. Far more broadly, this refers to the constant development of improved standards and rules of fairness for all of management's dealings with its employees, and then—and most importantly—finding constantly improved ways to ensure that the rules are scrupulously adhered to.

Organizations with past traditions of paternalism and operating under the pressures of heavy work loads are often derelict in this. Due process in a diplomatic establishment means, therefore, not only that the ground rules of a diplomat-employee's life are fairly drawn, but that he can count on their being followed.

§

Preoccupation with due process, and this talk of formidable employee-management relations systems and elaborate grievance structures, all have a strange ring to diplomats of an earlier time and tradition. The reformers, they say, are turning the U.S. diplomatic service "into the Teamsters' union, by God!" The State Department has become a haven for crybabies, the "grieve-yard of the Foreign Service." And with these charges come assertions, repeatedly expressed, that such developments inevitably undermine the basic and essential discipline of any diplomatic service.

But in the modern era this discipline cannot be maintained through a perpetuation of the paternalism and the tyrannies, however masked and genteel, of the past. On the contrary, the only effective way to assure a disciplined service, in this day and age, is to make sure that its basic safeguards for fairness to all are apparent to all.

The critics come not from this quarter alone. Often louder and even more strident are voices from the other end of the spectrum, voices charging that the pace of change is too slow, that the steps that have been taken have not gone nearly far enough.

The debate on this side of the issue, too, has its share of flaws and superficialities. Young Turk movements, valuable as they are, are almost never altogether devoid of attention-gathering and ego massage, not to mention occasionally unwarranted convictions of infallibility. And just as some elders would put the clock back if they could, some young would move it precipitously forward, without first understanding the intricacies of its mechanism.

The fact that debate can be marred in this way should never obscure its value as an instrument of modernization in the human-relations area. And the fact that out of it, and out of the operations of the employee-management relations system, arises a certain tumult from time to time—a tumult quite unseemly by earlier standards of diplomatic decorum—should not be a cause for dismay. Controversy is an integral part of progress. There have been many years in diplomatic establishments when there has been very little tumult and very little progress.

§

A final human-relations question, meriting special note, concerns a key group not even on the payroll.

One of the most obvious and important affirmative facts of diplomatic life is that, far more than in many professions, a wife can share, and play a significant role, in her husband's work. The job, particularly abroad, rather than separating them as it does in so many walks of life, brings them constantly together. Anyone who knows even the least about diplomacy knows what invaluable support an effective diplomatic wife can be to her husband, and how much the performance of any diplomatic institution depends on the cumulative contributions of its distaff side.

In most diplomatic institutions it is occasionally forgotten that wives are not on the payroll, that their invaluable contributions to embassy activities are made because they wish to make them, and not because these contributions can be requested by anyone who is their husbands' superior or who is the wife of their husbands' superior.

Officers in a diplomatic establishment are part of a chain of command. Their spouses are not. Younger wives must not feel pressure to serve as ladies in waiting, or otherwise be at the beck and call, of the wife of the ambassador or of any other wife whose husband happens to have a more senior place than her own husband in the embassy hierarchy.

A few wives in a diplomatic community probably will wish to focus exclusively on family responsibilities, or on taking courses at the local university, or on being a painter or writer, or on otherwise concentrating full time on their "own thing." Experience has shown that they will do this, regardless of the pressures put upon them by an informal but sometimes very potent distaff chain of command. A wife has every right to follow her own interests, and to follow them exclusively if she wishes, as long as these are consistent with the rules of the country in which she resides. Neither she nor her husband should have to resist pressure in order for her to be able to do this.

Experience has also shown that the percentage of wives in an embassy community who opt completely out of embassy representational, charitable, and other activities will be very small. Effective ambassadorial wives rarely want for support for the often incredibly heavy schedule of activities they conduct. This is so, not because the more "junior" wives feel obligated to help, but because they genuinely want to. They want to help because of their respect and affection for the ambassadress, and because of their belief that the activities are useful and important. Their help will not be diminished in any important way by the existence of a well-understood "wives' liberation policy" established to guard against the relatively few, but occasionally notable, tyrannies of the past. In fact, such a policy strengthens the flow of this vital distaff support by clearly establishing the true basis on which it rests.

It is in connection with her husband's representational role that a wife's support for, and participation in, his work is most apparent. Social contacts play an important part in the work of all diplomats, and representational activities are a key part of the job for which he is paid.

But again it is the officer who is paid, not his spouse. A diplomatic service has a right to expect that this part of the job will be done well, and this in turn will often depend in no small part on the supporting performance of his wife. But the obligation flows from the diplomat to his employer. If his wife lets him down, this will not likely help his career because his performance may suffer in an important professional area. The degree of support, or lack of it, supplied by a wife to her diplomat-husband, however, is a private matter between husband and wife, not an official matter between employer and wife.

This leads inevitably to the question of whether a wife's performance, often so critical to the effective performance of a diplomat and so important in the overall work of an embassy, should be referred to in the annual evaluation report concerning her diplomat-husband.

The answer must regrettably be in the negative. It is regrettable because it is so difficult even to begin to repay or even recognize the selfless contributions of so many diplomatic wives. And one of the few ways that it has in small measure been done is through the inclusion in this report each year of explicit laudatory comments on the effectiveness of her role. Not only did this practice in the past provide her with some recognition, it gave her the added satisfaction of knowing that what she was doing was directly helping her husband to advance in his career.

The difficulty is that if mention of a wife's performance is permitted in such reports, the absence of such comments provides a not very subtle tool to pressure the wife who wishes to go her own way. In an era which attaches importance to wives' being independent, equal human beings in their own right, and not simply adjuncts of their husbands, this weapon for conformity must be foreclosed.

This does not mean, of course, that wives who contribute so much must become "nonpersons" in the eyes of the government they serve. Alert foreign offices (and the diplomats' own professional organizations) will find other ways to identify and honor their contributions and achievements. This must be done, however, in channels entirely separate from those governing their husbands' ratings and promotions.

"Two for the price of one" has long been a slogan in which the diplomatic profession has taken much pride. To the extent that it honors selfless, voluntary, and invaluable distaff contributions to diplomatic life, it is pride well taken. The standards of a modern age require, however, that it never be used to camouflage exploitation, or to perpetuate in even the most limited sense any suggestion of secondary status or discriminatory treatment.

§

Building a modern human-relations system, as has been said, is not a pioneering experience; it has been done in many institutions before. It will be the management gap, rather than the human-relations gap, which will, in the end, be the more difficult for diplomatic establishments to close. Building a modernly managed diplomatic establishment appropriately designed to meet the demands of the modern era has not been done before. Breaking new ground is always the more difficult task.

There are some who argue that the best device to accomplish this is the periodic appointment of the blue-ribbon commission of outside experts. These experts, backed up by competent professional staffs and a year or two of intensive study, make a series of recommendations to the secretary or foreign minister who, with the aid of his top management officials, then imposes those recommendations he agrees with on the rest of the organization.

This is the classical method of bringing significant reforms to government bureaucracies. It brings an objective outside professional viewpoint to the problem, and over the years much good has been accomplished by it. It is a device which can and should, at few-year intervals, be used over and over again.

The trouble is that change-resistant bureaucracies outlast secretaries, foreign ministers, and politically appointed top managements who leave office before many of the reforms they sponsor can be fully and permanently implanted. Therefore, the commission is not a tool of reform that can be relied upon exclusively.

Another method, recently developed, is to launch a major broadly mandated effort from within the establishment. Rather than appointing a board of outside experts, an extensive series of task forces staffed by the diplomats themselves are given essentially the same task an outside blue-ribbon commission or panel would have. Such task forces should first review the unimplemented recommendations that inevitably lie buried in the massive dust-covered reports of earlier, more conventional, outside reform commission efforts. Often, the most valuable result of an internal task force effort will not be the new ideas they produce, but the impetus they supply for implementation of earlier recommendations.

They are designed for more than that, however. Internal task forces must examine every weakness of their service, and if they are honest with themselves they will know more about these than outsiders ever can. In the search for remedies they must tap all the expertise they can find, in and outside of their service. If they will take a thorough and open-minded look at their shortcomings, if they will search out all the relevant management experience in other institutions, public and private, if they will turn to outside management experts for help wherever they can get it, then because of the special insights they can bring to their work they are in the end in the best position of any to draw up the most effective and relevant solutions to their management problems.

Although the work of internal task forces cannot perhaps claim the same degree of objectivity generally ascribed to outside blue-ribbon commissions, it has a balancing advantage of considerable significance. Self-criticism is much less resented than the criticism of outsiders, even when that self-criticism is more severe and far-reaching. Even more important, the job of implementing recommendations proceeds more easily when the recommendations come not from outsiders, but from the very people who must put them into effect.

But valuable as is the periodic use of both the outside commission and the internal task force, neither is the basic answer to the question of how best to ensure continuing modernization in diplomacy's management areas.

That answer lies rather in the daily performance of the diplomats themselves. It is not a problem which can be worked on periodically, for it requires a constant and sustained effort. It can only come when all diplomats are prepared in their daily work to devote the same interest and emphasis to management tools and techniques they have been prepared to give to diplomacy's more traditional skills.

§

The discussion of management capabilities brings to a close the examination, in this and preceding chapters, of the four basic personal qualities and the ten professional core skills that are the essential equipment of the modern diplomat. To recapitulate, the core qualities are: 1) integrity, 2) discretion, 3) energy, and 4) self-discipline. The core skills have encompassed the ability to 1) report accurately, 2) report discriminately, 3) negotiate effectively, 4) analyze objectively, 5) speak persuasively, 6) master foreign tongues, 7) react effectively and resourcefully to unexpected situations, 8) develop sound creative policy choices and make wise recommendations regarding these choices, 9) effectively support national commercial interests, and 10) be a sound manager with a sophisticated understanding of modern management tools and systems.

Each of these fourteen essentials is difficult enough to master in its own right, and surely their collective mastery is a formidable task indeed. In fact, in contemplating this challenge, one is reminded of Clemenceau's remark at Versailles concerning a list of quite different purpose, but of similar length. "God gave us the ten commandments," declared the once famous tiger of French politics, "and we broke them. Wilson gives us fourteen points; we shall see."

Because they are so difficult to master, what we will see with respect to diplomacy's fourteen points will often be disappointing. But the professional will understand that, taken together, they constitute the essential modern infrastructure of his craft. He will regard that difficulty as a challenge, not a deterrent. He will devote a lifetime to the mastery of each, knowing that only in this way can he meet the critical responsibilities that the times place upon him.

CHAPTER THIRTEEN

Fools from Florence: Problems Old

IT IS UNFORTUNATE THAT the government of the United States cannot award knighthoods, or some other equally prestigious titles which carry no duties. With this somewhat startling thought to American ears, it is time to turn from problems of more recent origin to consider one that has bedeviled American diplomacy almost from its beginnings.

Apparently the thirst for titles is a universal one. In any event, it is by no means limited to those nations with knighthoods to confer. But the latter nations can meet this craving without simultaneously saddling themselves with an unqualified job incumbent. In short, they can award a knighthood, and not an embassy.

It is also a discouraging commentary on America's appreciation of the importance of its diplomatic arm to note that the effort to eliminate the spoils system from the American diplomatic service has historically been allowed to lag considerably behind similar efforts respecting almost all other important elements of the federal government. The result is that each succeeding administration in Washington has found the world of American embassies to be a happy hunting ground in which to reward those to whom political obligations have been felt. These obligations have generally arisen from past services to the party, notably, but by no means exclusively, in the area of substantial financial campaign contributions.

Generation after generation of United States diplomatic institutions abroad, not to mention long-suffering host governments, have often been seriously burdened by leaders who have been subprofessional, and occasionally far worse. The age of "bought" commissions for incompetent generals ended in the British Army long ago. In a sense, however, the American diplomatic service has remained to this day in the era of the Charge of the Light Brigade.

It is, of course, an unwise practice, and one which de Callières eloquently warned against many years ago. In his early-eighteenth-century classic on diplomacy, he tells us a story which unhappily is not without relevance to this day:

> The late Duke of Tuscany, who as a remarkably wise and enlightened prince, once complained to the Venetian Ambassador, who stayed overnight with him on the journey to Rome, that the Republic of Venice had sent as a resident at his court a person of no value, possessing neither judgment nor knowledge nor even an attractive personal quality. "I am not surprised," said the Ambassador in reply; "We have many fools in Venice." Whereupon the Grand Duke retorted, "We also have fools in Florence, but we take care not to export them."

And again, campaigning on the same subject, de Callières declares:

> The veriest fool would not entrust the command of an Army to a man whose sole badge of merit was his successful eloquence in a court of law or his adroit practice of the courtier's art in the palace. All are agreed military command must be earned by long service in the Army. In the same manner it should be regarded as folly to entrust the conduct of negotiations to an untrained amateur, unless he has conspicuously shown in some other walk of life the qualities and knowledge necessary for the practice of diplomacy.

Through the years this problem has persisted, but excesses have gradually produced a degree of reform, tardy and incomplete but by no means unimpressive.

In the American case, there is almost no political penetration of consequence in the diplomatic service in any position below the rank of ambassador. While administrations occasionally eye consul generalships, these remain by and large inviolate. Deputy chiefs of missions at embassies and all those diplomats reporting to them are career officials. When a political ambassador comes to an embassy, he may bring a personal assistant of temporary tenure from outside the diplomatic service, but otherwise he will be surrounded by a solid core of professionals whose ranks generally remain effectively resistant to noncareer penetration.

To say that the only political leakage into the system is at its very top is, of course, to highlight the fact that this leakage comes at a vulnerable place indeed. Substantial elimination of the spoils principle from the remainder of the system is, however, an accomplishment of considerable importance.

This leakage at the top is significant but not overwhelming. In recent years, over the course of several administrations, the percentage of political appointees in American ambassadorial ranks has run at about 30 per cent. About 70 per cent of all ambassadorial appointments have gone to career diplomats. This figure, however, has fluctuated from year to year. There have been times when career officials have occupied more than 80 per cent of the U.S. ambassadorial positions, and on one occasion, at least, that figure had sunk to the neighborhood of 51 per cent. The number of career officials tends to be at its lowest in the first years of a new administration and to rise as the administration grows older.

A beleaguered State Department, often with the support of its secretary, deputy secretary, and other senior political appointees, has learned over the years to fight a dogged battle against prospective appointments of the more flagrant kind. It is not always a battle which is won, but it is not one which has always been lost either.

While most of the time it is a lonely effort, occasionally valuable help is forthcoming from editorial and congressional sources. The key has been, however, a strong secretary who is prepared to take on the patronage dispensers in all instances where departmental subordinates have been unable to turn aside an unfit candidacy.

It is important to remember that by no means are all outside appointments contrary to the nation's interest. The saga of noncareer appointees has all too often produced the inadequate as well as, on occasion, the disgraceful and bizarre. But it has also brought valuable skills, insights, and perspectives from other walks of American life, and it has produced a number of solid performances, ranging from the adequate-plus to the excellent. Most important of all, a few noncareer appointees have proven to be truly outstanding performers, at least the equal of the very best the career ranks have ever produced.

The earlier examples are well known. Benjamin Franklin, John Adams, Charles Francis Adams, Joseph H. Choate, to name but a few, set standards all diplomats must surely honor. The tradition continues to this day, with such men as David Bruce and Ellsworth Bunker having proven, through a series of brilliant performances in many exacting assignments, to be the match of any diplomats America has produced in this century.

There is nothing the matter, *per se,* with the concept of appointing persons from outside of career ranks to top diplomatic assignments. A diplomatic career is not the only one which can produce successful diplomats, as experience has shown again and again. The core skills of diplomacy are not diplomacy's exclusive patent. They are required in many walks of life, and they can be, and often are, learned elsewhere.

A few judiciously chosen outsiders can broaden and enrich any diplomatic service. Moreover, any president and his secretary of state must have a degree of flexibility to go outside the ranks of the diplomatic service to find exactly the right envoy to deal with a particular situation. The career principle need not, and should not, be carried to the hundredth percentile.

As a political appointee of both parties and for many years, I am nevertheless increasingly convinced that the percentile of exceptions should be narrow indeed. For while very good diplomats can be recruited from outside the diplomatic life, both logic and experience argue that the man or woman who has spent a lifetime in diplomacy is a far better bet for an ambassadorial assignment than all but the most gifted outsiders. Over the years the Bunkers and Bruces have been but a handful, and those of the still very valuable next rank but a few handfuls more. A policy of making at least 95 per cent career assignments should still be adequate, therefore, to provide for this occasional but essential and invaluable infusion from without. After watching the appointee process for many years, and in four assignments at rather close range, I am persuaded that a lesser percentile will almost inevitably present a too inviting target for abuse.

More important than a change in percentages is a change in the philosophy behind them. The historic acceptance of ambassadorial plums as a part of the patronage process is simply no longer good enough. An individual should not be barred from a high diplomatic post because he has made a financial contribution to the party of his choice or played an effective political role in the service of that party. This should be irrelevant one way or the other. Outsiders should be chosen only on the basis of the special background and skills they bring to the specific job at hand.

Politically motivated appointments should be abolished. Non-career appointments should not be barred altogether; if wisely chosen, they can enrich and strengthen the performance of a diplomatic service. But such appointments should be kept to an absolute minimum; and when one is made, a convincing explanation must be offered as to why in that instance it makes sense to turn away from the available pool of reliable and experienced professionals.

Anyone who has been in past struggles to hold the career percentage up to 70 per cent can have no illusions about how difficult such advances will be to accomplish—or as to how equally difficult, once achieved, they will be to maintain.

It is, of course, essential to get away from the practice of expecting rich ambassadors to help meet the expenses, particularly the representational expenses, of some of the costlier posts from their own pockets. It is essential to make clear that no post anywhere in the service is barred to any career diplomat because of an absence of private means. This is an archaic and reprehensible situation, left over from traditions of artistocratic government, totally out of keeping with modern concepts.

It would be well also to take a leaf from the procedures the bar associations have established for the nomination of candidates for judicial posts. Although the members of the American Foreign Service Association are in a different relationship to the President from members of the American Bar Association, this should not be an insurmountable obstacle to the establishment of a panel of distinguished career diplomats whose responsibility, like that of their lawyer counterparts, would be to pass on the fitness of those nominated to lead diplomatic missions abroad. While it would be preferable to have this panel manned, at least in part, by active-duty professionals, distinguished retired professionals could also perform this function. Its main purpose, of course, would be to screen out unqualified noncareer candidacies, but it should be prepared to pass on career candidates as well.

For just as noncareer appointments are not *per se* unacceptable, neither are all career appointments appropriate. In the case of a career diplomat, a review panel should assure itself that his attainments place him in the front rank of his profession and that he has not subsequently run out of steam, or slipped markedly past his peak.

A variation of abuse in the political appointee area is the practice, occasionally followed by some countries, of exiling to diplomatic assignments abroad political rivals to the regime currently in authority. Here the purpose of such appointments is not to reward someone owed a political debt, but to get rid of someone who represents a political threat. Obviously, such a distrusted appointee cannot be a true representative of the government which has dispatched him, and such a practice perverts the whole rationale of why diplomatic hospitality is extended. Receiving states should firmly refuse agreement to such appointments.

§

Another long-standing problem of a quite different character still lingers to plague diplomacy—the ever-present hazard of catching "localitis." This is a traditional disease, well recognized by diplomats. Even so, it is not always properly guarded against.

The problem is that in addition to speaking for the interests of his own country, a diplomat's responsibility is to ensure that his own government understands the attitudes and concerns of the host government as they bear on the relations between the two states—and it often becomes a fine line, indeed, between explanation and advocacy. It is normal and commendable for a diplomat to develop an interest and sympathy for the nation where he has been assigned. The fatal flaw, however, is to forget that he is sent abroad to represent the interests of his own country to the host country, and not vice versa.

It is a problem which comes especially to the fore when, as is sometimes the case, with new countries or ones inexperienced in international affairs, a diplomat stationed there feels that his host country's own diplomats are not adequately explaining the legitimate reasons impelling the host government to act and think as it does. In these circumstances, the tendency to focus on explaining host-government views to his own, rather than the other way around, becomes most acute.

The procedural theory behind the conduct of diplomatic relations between two states is that each state deals with the other primarily through its embassy in that state's capital. Thus, if country X wishes to make a point to country Y, it asks its embassy in country Y to call at the country Y foreign office and the message will be conveyed through that channel. Subsequently, if the theory holds, the answer will be delivered by country Y's embassy to the foreign office of country X.

It is a theory most honored in the breach. Officials of country X may initiate the exchange not via its own embassy, but by simply calling in an official of the country Y embassy and delivering their message in that way. Often a country will initiate its message through both channels simultaneously. On the other hand, if the original country X message is conveyed through its own embassy in country Y, that country may choose to reply through the channel by which the message originally came, that is, back through country Y's embassy.

In any event, and theory aside, sooner or later a "center of gravity" begins to develop with respect to the procedural side of the two countries' relationship. The locus of that relationship tends to center in one of the two embassies involved. One of the two embassies will find that it is both the primary conveyor and receiver of communications between the two states. The other embassy, while being kept informed of the exchanges and advising its parent country on the implications involved, finds itself somewhat on the sidelines.

This does not need to happen, but it often does. Again, it is a situation where the problem of localitis may somewhat understandably arise. An embassy which knows it is the center of gravity, and knows its opposite number embassy is somewhat "out of it," may feel a more than usual obligation to be sure that the host country's side of things is fully understood back home.

Localitis can infect diplomats of all levels—from third secretaries to ambassadors—but it is most dangerous, of course, among ambassadors. Politically appointed noncareer ambassadors have occasionally had a special proclivity to become apologists for the countries to which they have been sent. It is discouraging to note that career ambassadors, also, can be surprisingly susceptible to this disease. All diplomats must guard against it.

While diplomats at all times should obviously show a decent respect for the manners, traditions, and customs of their host country, they should never overdo this to the point of "going native." In countries where Arab garb is still the custom, he does not have to get dressed up like Lawrence of Arabia to be a successful envoy. Or, to take a more subdued example, he need not affect a derby hat in London. In fact, the adoption of such practices is as good a warning as a home office will ever have that the time has more than come to move such representatives along.

There is a reverse side of localitis. Occasionally a diplomat, because of unfortunate personal experiences or for some other reason, develops an intense aversion to his host country. Antilocalitis can become so pronounced that it colors and distorts his judgment on all matters concerning it.

It is surprisingly present, in a less extreme form, in far too may diplomats. The basic rule is that neither admiration of his host country nor lack of it must ever be allowed to color a diplomat's judgment respecting his own country's interest. Nor must it disfigure in any other way the objectivity and professional character of his performance.

§

A further variant of this problem of critical attitude merits comment. This is the criticism which comes from a diplomat who feels himself to be a bona fide friend and admirer of his host country and believes himself recognized as such by its citizens.

Because he assumes his friendship and admiration are well known, he can find himself offering the type of criticism of his hosts he might express at home with respect to his own country's shortcomings. But it is a risky business, as he will soon learn when he finds such remarks being taken out of context. The fact that such remarks come from a "friend" has little effect on the damage they can do to his standing with his hosts. This is a problem which diplomats who have served for an especially long time in a country and who have come in effect to consider it as a second home must be particularly on their guard against.

In many situations this rudimentary stricture is breached, often unthinkingly. Speaking of one of the more common of these, Sir Ernest Satow warned diplomats of an earlier era that "The head of a mission should be careful that the affairs, the manners, and customs of the country in which he is residing are not criticized at his table. What he or his guests may say on such subjects is sure to be reported to his disadvantage. A [local citizen] occasionally makes disparaging remarks about his own country. A diplomat should think twice before agreeing with them."

§

Good manners are useful to anybody. They are a requirement of particular importance for all diplomats. A professional who allows himself to forget this is simply no diplomat.

The more difficult, complex, and emotionally charged the issues with which the diplomat must deal, the more essential good manners and polite dialogue become. The same principle is enforced in parliamentary bodies, and for the same reason. The elaborate courtesies that legislators extend to one another in debate, especially when the debate is intense, are often the subject of parody and ridicule. Such introductory phrases as "I say to my friend, and he is my good friend ..." have, nevertheless, been maintained through the years because they have served, and continue to serve, a useful purpose. Important discussions, whether of an adversary character or not, can be difficult enough without being additionally burdened by verbally augmented personal antagonism.

As the undiplomatic reply of the Spartans to the visiting ambassadors from Samos indicated, this was not a principle universally recognized in the early days of intercourse between peoples. Charles Thayer reports, as another memorable instance of the same point, a famous postwar foreign minister speaking with approval to his diplomatic colleagues of a communication sent several centuries earlier by his countryman to a nearby head of state. In its early lines this message termed the addressee "a comrade of the accursed devil" and after continuing for some time in that vein came to its close in a manner consistent with the vituperative tone it had employed throughout. Today, diplomatic notes generally end with the somewhat archaic but gracious phrase, "Accept, Excellency, assurances of my highest consideration." This one ended, "Kiss our ass."

Even in modern times, the requirement for careful courtesy in international communication is not always met. Stimulated by outrage or exasperation, or simply by the instincts of a boor and a bully, lapses still occur, although generally these are more muted than those examples from earlier times. And even those states that generally know and do better can occasionally be remiss. It was not, after all, so many years ago that an out-of-patience British foreign minister was heard to exclaim of an American note, "This reads like they still think they are talking to George the Third!"

To avoid this type of situation, the language of diplomacy has, through the centuries, developed its own style of restraint and understatement. As a young diplomat I still remember my amazement in hearing an American secretary of state, long experienced in diplomacy, privately characterize a particularly outrageous and hostile action against the United States as "very nearly an unfriendly act."

Diplomats learn that phrases such as "an unfriendly act," "cannot remain indifferent to," "views with concern," or "views with grave concern," and their like have a special meaning when used by nations in their dealings with one another. Understatement, in fact, has become such a trademark of the profession that long ago the old saying was invented that:

> If a lady says "no," she means "perhaps."
> If a lady says "perhaps," she means "yes."
> If a lady says "yes," she is no lady!
> and
> If a diplomat says "yes," he means "perhaps."
> If a diplomat says "perhaps," he means "no."
> If a diplomat says "no," he is no diplomat!

Of course, understatement can be overdone. And overdone to the point where to avoid one sin of diplomacy an even greater one, that of misleading, is perpetrated instead. It is essential that diplomats ensure that their exact meaning is understood, and true professionals will always employ language which is both polite and clear. In essence, the objective must always be "*La vérité dite, quelquefois avec force, toujours avec grâce.*"

Of course, diplomats and host country officials who have become close friends will often, in conversations where no others are present, take liberties with diplomacy's rules, and employ a mutual and unvarnished bluntness which can be very useful. Even here the diplomat would be well advised to remember the advice of one of America's most distinguished commentators on the dealings of nations with one another. "The sincerity of a government must never be called into question," wrote John Bassett Moore. "Facts may be denied, deductions examined, disapproved and condemned, without just cause of offense; but no impeachment of the integrity of the government in its reliance on the correctness of its own views can be permitted. . . ." This was written for an earlier and far different era of diplomacy. It remains sound advice to this day.

§

The diplomat abroad should always remember that despite the official character of his role, he is essentially a guest in the country in which he resides. This means that while certain obligations flow to him because of his status as a guest, others are very obviously owed by him in return.

Paramount among these is the obligation scrupulously to observe both the letter and the spirit of local laws and regulations, including specifically those related to automobile traffic and parking. Diplomatic immunity is not license, and those who use it as such abuse the hospitality which has been extended to them. They strain rather than improve relations, and reveal themselves of a character and habits generally unsuited to their profession.

Chiefs of diplomatic missions have a particular responsibility in this area. Through the force of their leadership and, more important, by their personal example, they must ensure that all in their mission zealously adhere to the highest possible standards in this critically important area of personal conduct. Those who are not prepared to meet these standards should be weeded out of the profession.

A chief of mission has a related responsibility because of the import and other privileges accorded to him and to the members of his embassy by the host government. These represent official exceptions to the normal rules and requirements of the host government. Those who are accorded them have an obvious obligation to see that they are employed honorably, and only for the purpose for which they are granted. A chief of mission and all his colleagues have a clear obligation to make certain that there is no violation of that trust.

Customs exemptions have long been a source of difficulty. De Callières, writing of the late 1600's and early 1700's, reports, "The Spanish Government was obliged a few years ago to regulate those privileges for all foreign envoys residing in Madrid, and the Republic of Genoa found it necessary to adopt the same somewhat humiliating precautions in order to prevent diplomats from engaging in illicit traffic." The problem, unfortunately, continues to crop up to this day, and chiefs of mission will find that wrongdoing can come from both embassy colleagues of his own nationality and from the embassy's host nation employees.

The latter, known as "local employees," are the forgotten men and women of diplomacy, serving the diplomatic process the world over with distinction, but with very little recognition, and often with even less in the way of proper remuneration.

Like any other group, they can have their few who are corrupt. An area of particular concern for the leadership of any embassy, therefore, must be where the same local employees operate the customs-exemption procedures year after year, while their foreign supervisory personnel constantly turn over as traditional two- and four-year tours keep coming to an end. Most local employees in this situation are scrupulous in the performance of their duties. Experience has shown, however, that where there has been difficulty, either through advertence or inadvertence, this occasionally has been its locus.

Human nature, of course, makes no distinction with regard to such matters, either as between nationalities within an embassy, or as between embassies throughout the world. Chiefs of mission, therefore, should always, as one of their early steps upon arriving at a post, review the procedures, which all missions have, to guard against misuse of all privileges granted by the host government. It is his duty to ensure that these procedures are both effectively designed and properly implemented.

§

Through the centuries, and to this day, the tradition of gift-giving has become hopelessly entangled with traditions of hospitality. It takes no great judgment or skill to reject a gift offered for improper reasons, but it is quite another matter to turn away, with skill and graciousness, gifts offered out of hospitality and friendship. In fact, as every experienced diplomat knows, it is often impossible to do this, particularly in certain countries where traditions of gift-giving run deep, and the rejection of a gift cannot be understood.

Yet most diplomatic services quite properly seek to enforce prohibitions against gift-receiving. The following instructions issued to American officials in 1838 can be taken as a random sampling of the guidance which has been in force in many services through the years. American officials were not, in these aged instructions, without the consent of Congress to "accept, under any circumstances, presents of any kind whatever" from officials of foreign states. It is still the basic guidance that all diplomats should follow.

But realities intervene, and it is often impossible to do this without giving offense. Many states have developed a fallback rule which permits a diplomat to receive a gift in situations where he feels that to do otherwise will constitute a serious breach of diplomatic etiquette. He then must turn the gift over to his own government, where it is stored in an official warehouse.

The trouble with this solution is that warehouses are soon filled to overflowing. Additionally, of course, it is in essence a silly nonuse of often valuable and useful things.

Government rules sometimes provide for gifts stored in this way to be given back to those officials who received them once they have retired from public service. This, of course, means that the rules do allow a diplomat to receive and keep valuable gifts. The fact that he cannot use them until retirement detracts very little from their ultimate value and usefulness to him.

Some governments develop an increasingly generous *de minimus* rule. The *de minimus* rule, in effect, says that the no-gift prohibition does not extend to trifles; that is, to gifts of such limited value that it makes no sense to bring them under the prohibitory rules.

As the warehouses fill to overflowing, however, governments find themselves upping their definitions of *de minimus* to cut down on the inflow into these official holding facilities. Before very long, *de minimus* gets defined as a price range which by any standards, other than those of harassed warehouse keepers, is no longer truly *de minimus*.

Honest diplomats, therefore, develop supplementary devices to prevent their public office from being a source of private benefit.

For instance, where gifts cannot be refused, they can be appraised and a gift of equal value can be made, funded from the diplomat's own pocket. Or he can make a charitable contribution in that amount, over and above his normal annual charitable gifts. Or, if it can be done discreetly and the gift is of an appropriate nature, he can pass it along to a charitable or educational institution. Or, again, if it is of an appropriate nature, he can put it on display at the embassy residence or office, and upon his departure from post leave it behind as a permanent item in the embassy's inventory.

Or yet again, if the gift came in the form of a food item, it can be passed on to a charitable institution. Or, if it is food or alcoholic beverages, both favorites at Christmas time, these can be put to good use at subsequent official embassy functions.

It takes only a little effort in imagination and resourcefulness for a diplomat to ensure against personal profit where his government's rules, for the practical reasons just cited, have become too lax. But unless and until the day finally comes when it is universally recognized that gifts to a diplomat are an embarrassment—and are, therefore, no longer proffered—he is obligated scrupulously to make this effort in order to ensure that, even in this often minor way, he never personally profits from his official position. Petty graft is petty graft, whether it takes place around a city hall or in an embassy.

§

Embassies tend to remain, with respect to their internal structures and ways of doing things, as their nations' last outposts of feudalism. Authority is notably centered in the person of the ambassador, and there is still a marked degree of protocol deference paid to him, both outside and inside his embassy.

This deference originated in the days when kings considered themselves anointed by God, and when their ambassadors, as their direct representatives, expected to be treated as nearly as august personages. This rationale has, of course, disappeared, but the deference tends to remain. The ambassador still represents his head of state and, more than that, his embassy colleagues consider that through the office he holds, he more than anyone among them symbolizes and represents their country.

Deference of this kind can erode perspective and more than one ambassador has come a cropper because of it. The classic advice to take one's job seriously but never oneself is nowhere more applicable than to chiefs of diplomatic missions. Years ago one of my most distinguished predecessors as the State Department's chief administrative and personnel officer wrote a "Dutch uncle" letter to an embassy leader whose proconsul ways had come to his attention. That letter concluded with the blunt admonition never to forget "that a touch of humility never hurt the performance of an Ambassador of the United States." Neither, one should add, does a sense of humor. Both are reminders that all ambassadors should have tattooed on their hides.

An ambassador's authority has a more modern and realistic rationale, unrelated to kings. With so many competing interests and priorities emanating from across the spectrum of his government structure back home, it is essential that embassy activities be coordinated by one commanding voice.

This is so even though the representatives, on the embassy scene, of the various headquarters' agencies are generally far less competitive with one another than are their parent organizations at home. In the field, the representatives of the various agencies tend to join together and to back each other in their battles with their respective headquarters. This is not always the case, but it usually is. Even so, if the ambassador did not have the authority he does, each embassy would soon become an open invitation to anarchy.

But if the deference is partly understandable, and the authority wholly so, the end result still causes concern. While the use of the word "feudal" a moment ago is perhaps overstatement, there is always the danger that this combination of deference and authoritarianism will stultify creative thinking.

It is the chief of mission's obvious duty to use his prestige and authority to see that fresh winds blow throughout his embassy community. He should encourage original thinking and conflicting ideas, insisting only that they rest on a factually sound base and that they be logically developed. When they crop up, he should take it as a compliment to his leadership, and he should be pleased to report dissenting views, along with his own comments respecting them, back to headquarters. In fact, if he doesn't willingly do this, the dissenter should be able, as a matter of right, to go back through a separate dissent channel established for just this purpose.

§

Diplomats at all levels pride themselves on doing their homework, but it is surprising how often this is neglected in one essential area.

The basic relations between two states are not, to repeat the phrase of Sir Harold Nicolson, a matter of conversation. What their respective representatives are saying to each other at any particular time is, of course, of great importance, but the basic infrastructure of the relationship is to be found collectively set out in the treaties and other written agreements which the two nations have negotiated and signed. While diplomats at a post pride themselves on their knowledge of their host country's history, traditions, customs, and on being informed on where the current dialogue with their own country stands, far too many have but the most casual acquaintance with the range of basic documents that fundamentally govern the two nations' relationships.

Collected in one looseleaf notebook should be all consular treaties, treaties of friendship, commerce, and navigation, security treaties, status-of-forces agreements, exchanges of diplomatic notes, and the like which govern relations in any fundamental way. All officers coming to a post, and all those assigned to the country desk back home, should as a first order of business come to know these key documents as they do the backs of their hands.

It is a good idea, also, to find the time to go back into the files and see what ambassadors and embassy reporting officers of an earlier day were reporting back home. Certain elements both in a nation's character and in its bilateral relations with a particular state tend to persist. Earlier commentary may or may not have been correct, or, if correct at the time, may or may not still be correct. But those who came later, while obviously not bound by earlier thinking, should be exposed to it for whatever insight and historical background it can provide. This earlier reporting tends, however, to be a prominent area of busy modern diplomacy's benign neglect.

§

Another area, not altogether neglected but not usually receiving the constant emphasis it should, is the obligation, spoken of earlier, that the more senior and experienced diplomats in an embassy have to instruct in a systematic way the more junior and inexperienced. Some senior officers take this responsibility very seriously, but far too many expect the young to learn pretty much by osmosis, augmented by an occasional word of praise or complaint.

What is required is a sustained effort in this area by all senior officials. This does not mean organized lectures; it does mean a senior officer constantly explaining what he is doing, why he is doing it the way he is, and what alternative means or tactics were considered before he made the choice he did. It means, for example, an ambassador bringing as many of his junior officers as possible in on his briefing sessions when he is preparing for an important meeting with a host country president, prime minister, or foreign minister. It means, as noted earlier, bringing them in when negotiating tactics are being discussed, even when they are not directly involved in the negotiations themselves. It means, in short, consciously and systematically inserting them into every learning situation available.

The obligation does not run just one way. Younger diplomats have an obligation also. Theirs is constantly to learn from the older experience and talent around them, regardless of whether their elders are consciously teaching or not.

As a young diplomat moves ahead in his career, he should systematically pattern his own developing style after those specific elements in the performance of a variety of senior officers which have most impressed him. The goal is, of course, to develop a matured style based on judicious borrowings from the best he has been exposed to along the way.

No new generation of diplomats can capture intact all the experience and skills of its predecessors' generation. In the diplomatic profession, as in anything else, each generation must go through a certain amount of previously well-plowed ground and learn from its own mistakes. But it does not have to be as extensive and redundant, and therefore as wasteful, a process as it usually is. And it will not be, if diplomacy's older generation will learn, more universally and more systematically, to meet its daily requirements to teach, as well as to do.

§

Implicit in the foregoing advice to the young is that capabilities within all human beings are uneven. The same principle holds true in reverse; for example, when a senior officer surveys the more junior hierarchy upon which he must rely to help meet his responsibilities. Within that hierarchy will surely be some who, because of an absence of talent or experience, do not do some things as well as a senior officer would like, or as well as he himself could do them.

The older official can live out his life blissfully overlooking his own shortcomings, but constantly frustrated by the inevitable short-comings of others. Or he can recognize the humbling but reassuring truth that never in his life will he meet someone who cannot perform in some area or in some way better than he can; that anyone who has the innate ability to pass stiff diplomatic service entrance exams can do many things well from the start, and that the key to effective leadership is to discover where the strengths of colleagues lie, and to place primary reliance upon them in those areas of their special competence.

§

Rules, procedures, and attitudes, often rather rigid, and largely historical in nature, still govern much of the conduct of diplomacy. The world of agreements, letters of credence and recall, first-person notes, *notes verbales*, aides-mémoire, precedence, "signing the book," leaving cards, introductory and farewell calls, and a host of other traditional customs remains an integral part of the profession.

To modern ears, these all have a markedly archaic ring, rituals designed for an earlier world of different character and pace. But each was designed to serve a specific, practical purpose in that earlier time, and to a surprising degree many are still notably functional today. In any event, they remain diplomacy's basic "rules of the road." And while diplomats may chafe under their occasional cumbersomeness, they will, if they are professionals, scrupulously adhere to them as long as the host government desires that they remain in force.

The problem, of course, is that not all of these inheritances are still useful. A few constitute empty and unnecessary burdens on either the diplomatic corps, or host government officials, or both. In such circumstances it is foolishness to continue to be governed by procedures which once made sense, but do so no longer. Some years ago, I was told by a senior American diplomat that I would find being an ambassador an "often interesting, occasionally ridiculous" business. The ridiculousness he referred to stems almost entirely from formalities and rigidities which have long outlived their relevance.

If a procedure becomes silly and out of date for a certain country, the diplomats there should seek to remove it. This should be done as a collective step, preferably under the leadership of the dean of the corps, and should only be accomplished if the host government also is persuaded to a similar view. Until this has been accomplished, it is important again to stress that professionals zealously abide by the rules as they are, and not as they would like them to be.

One area in which this latter stricture was doggedly, and on the whole rather admirably, violated by American diplomacy for many years had to do with the wearing of diplomatic uniforms. Getting dressed up in masses of gold braid has long seemed inappropriate for the representative of a republic which has prided itself from the start on its egalitarianism. While there have been exceptions, authorized and unauthorized, to the simple standards first set by Franklin at the French court, the United States government has persistently taken the view that diplomatic uniforms are to be shunned and that all its representatives, to use the words of an 1853 State Department instruction, should adhere instead "to the simple dress of an American citizen."

This policy had its critics, of course, and was often condemned as an attention-gathering form of reverse snobbism also inconsistent with republican principles. Joseph Choate, a successful last-century American diplomat in or out of uniform, is reported to have declared, "At a court this republican simplicity dodge of ours is the most impertinent piece of swagger in the world . . . not one human being in the room fails to notice the conspicuous character of their dress or to know that they are the modest and retiring American Ambassador."

Despite such an important advocate on the other side, the American tradition of no uniforms has continued to this day. And those on the side of no uniforms have not been without an eloquence of their own.

Legend has it that earlier in this century the last serious efforts to design and authorize an American diplomatic uniform failed when the then secretary of state's careful eye caught an artistic addition to the drawings of the uniform being proposed. These drawings had been sent up to him for approval through all the appropriate layers of State Department bureaucracy. Somewhere in that process, however, the papers had come across the desk of a resourceful opponent, who had taken the opportunity to put the effort into what he regarded as its proper perspective. Carefully he had inscribed, amid all the curlicues of the uniform's ornate design, a sprig of mistletoe on the seat of its pants.

The wearing of a uniform is no longer an issue in modern diplomacy. Some nations still have their representatives do so, but many have joined the American tradition and do not. And if secret envy once flowed from those who did not wear uniforms to those who did, the reverse is probably now the case. In fact, the modern price of these often still lavish costumes is such that many of their wearers must indeed now envy their colleagues in more modest attire.

It is still, however, generally a bad business, the uniform story notwithstanding, for diplomats to violate the contemporary practices of their profession. That story is a good one—best remembered as the exception which proves the rule.

§

Another, and particularly difficult, traditional problem area for all diplomats is the effective handling of their respective state departments or foreign ministries back home. Diplomats abroad soon find that this takes a surprisingly high percentage of their time and energy.

For not only is "the establishment of confidence and credit"—to use Nicolson's phrase—important as between an embassy and its host country's foreign office, it is equally essential between that embassy and its own home office. "No diplomat is less to be envied," wrote de Callières, "than he who finds himself at a foreign court bereft of the confidence of his own."

In addition to confidence, there must also be support. A diplomat simply cannot do his job if he is not kept currently and fully informed of all pertinent developments at home which affect his responsibilities, if his queries are not answered, and if his recommendations are not promptly acted upon. Without this support, host government officials will soon sense that he is not in a position to do his work, and he will promptly lose his standing and effectiveness with them. This will happen even more promptly, of course, if host officials sense that he has lost his government's confidence as well.

Given the vital importance then of headquarters' confidence and support, it is hardly surprising that wise diplomats work very hard indeed to achieve them both.

Confidence should be earned only through a consistent across-the-board performance which headquarters recognizes as meeting the highest standards of professional judgment and conduct. Eliciting effective support, while not totally unrelated to the standing an embassy and its leadership have at home, is essentially a quite different challenge.

This requires an ability to deal adroitly with a large bureaucracy, which is what most foreign offices have become, a challenge made even more difficult by having to conduct these dealings from far away. To compound the problem further, many embassies have themselves swollen into bureaucracies, which means the added complexities and frustrations of two bureaucracies dealing with each other. Given the seemingly endless number of clearances required on almost all important messages being sent to **an** embassy, it is a wonder that any reply ever comes on time or still makes any real sense after each clearance office has had a chance to reword it, prior to its dispatch.

Certainly the parties at each end of the cable traffic can irritate and disappoint each other, and at times rather drastically. When this happens, the temptation for an aggressive and strong-willed diplomat, or one with a low frustration tolerance, to let go with a blunt and ill-humored message to headquarters is a strong one indeed. The Duke of Wellington's alleged message to his higher headquarters in England during the Peninsula campaign is something of a classic in this regard. "My Lords," he is said to have declared, "I am determined to be governed by your instructions, so long as they remain within the reach of my comprehension."

Unless a diplomat considers himself a Wellington, this is not the recommended way to handle headquarters. Dealing with bureaucracies is not a visceral game; attacking the home office does not put people back there on one's side; and many years of observing sixth- and seventh-floor reactions have convinced me that intemperate messages rarely accomplish their objective. Instead, they almost always lead to a diminution of confidence in the sender.

A far better tactic is to deal with an unhelpful message by suppressing irritation and frustration, and then calmly setting out the problem the message creates from the vantage point of the recipient. The object of the return message is not to get backs up at home, but rather to put headquarters officials in the embassy's shoes, and to get them to perceive the requirements of the situation in the same light that the embassy does. If a calm and persuasive telegram, calculated to accomplish this, cannot be readily drafted, then there is strong reason to believe that the frustrations and anger were unjustified. If it can be, it will not always result in headquarters' changing its position, but it surely offers better prospects of accomplishing this than the dispatch of a Wellington-type message.

Generally speaking, the keys to obtaining effective headquarters support are a strong desk officer adept in handling bureaucracy, an enlightened understanding by embassy officials of headquarters' concerns and perspectives, logical persuasion and calm persistence, and—as has just been stressed—good manners.

Good manners are as necessary for the diplomat in his dealings with embassy-home office problems as they are for his dealings on the international scene. The reason is the same. For here, too, the problems can be sufficiently difficult on their own, without being augmented by unnecessary additional strains. A diplomat operating at either end of the embassy-home office axis who adds to these strains by a display of bad manners in his cable drafting bears watching. He has put his colleagues on notice that he is likely to misperform on the international scene as well.

Nothing more quickly clears the air and gets officials at both ends of the cables back on the same wave length concerning their respective needs and views than a trip back home by embassy officials, or vice versa. The resulting face-to-face conversations are invaluable for clearing up misunderstandings and merging perspectives. Embassies have yet to devise a better way periodically to refurbish their supporting structure.

§

Diplomats should seek an amicable and constructive rapport with their opposite-number embassy—that is, their host country's embassy back in their own capital. Distance inhibits what can be done and a range of differing circumstances will control the extent to which the two organizations have, or do not have, common purposes. The relationship should be cultivated, nevertheless, during respective visits home, or when other opportunities present, for the obvious reason that this opposite-number institution represents the other important anchor in the bilateral relationship between the two countries.

Another relationship of considerable importance for the overseas diplomat is that with his local private community of fellow citizens. It is his duty to support these private persons living overseas in a number of significant commercial and consular areas. If this is done with care and conscientiousness, the dividend in return can be substantial.

This is not, of course, a new truth. De Callières, writing in 1716, said it as well as anyone. "The better," he points out, that a diplomat's "relations are with his countrymen living abroad, the more surely will he discover how large are the reciprocal benefits to be gained by this, for it will often happen that unofficial persons receive information as it were by accident which may be of the utmost importance ... [and] unless good relations exist ... [the diplomat] may remain in ignorance of important facts."

§

A diplomat's representational duties have been briefly mentioned earlier, but this function merits attention in its own right, for representation remains a key part of any diplomat's job. Moreover it is a part of the job that is always with him. A negotiation sooner or later comes to an end, and it may be some time before a new one begins. Many other diplomatic activities have a similar rhythm of rising and falling activity. But for the conscientious diplomat, there can be no such interludes in the pursuit of his representational functions.

Representational responsibilities extend well beyond official, ceremonial, and social gatherings, although this is the context in which they are most often thought of. They come into play whenever a diplomat is doing anything, no matter how important or unimportant, that is seen by others in the country to which he is accredited. They require that, not just in his conduct on all public occasions, but in all contacts with host country officials, other resident diplomats, and local private citizens, he must at all times strive to be "representative" of what is the best and most admirable in the character of his countrymen. It specifically means that, on all such occasions, he must seek to represent his nation's highest standards in his display of knowledge, and in his commitment to decency, compassion, friend-liness, and hospitality. All this is, of course, a tall order, which no diplomat can really hope to fill. Persistently to attempt it, however, is a fundamental obligation of his calling.

The purpose of a diplomat's representational activity can be succinctly put. It is to earn for his country the respect and good will of all those he encounters. In the pursuit of this effort, of course, no diplomat can hope to influence any but a small portion of his host country's inhabitants, no matter how active and able his representa-tional activities. Nevertheless, if he designs the pattern of these activities with care, he can reach particularly important elements of the population, who can have, in turn, a disproportionate influence on the thinking of their countrymen.

The problem of properly focussing representational efforts is particularly important in official entertainment. Here nothing is more wasteful of a diplomat's energies and time than to allow himself to become trapped into a cycle of endlessly incurring, and repaying, social obligations—a cycle which develops its own momentum, and over which its participants exercise a minimum of influence. Nor are energy and time only wasted. So are the quarters provided by a diplomat's government in support of his representational efforts, so are the official entertainment funds, meager as they may be, which have also been provided for this purpose. Yet this cycle will entrap any unwary diplomat. The best way to avoid it is periodically to work out, each time for many months in advance, an entertainment "game plan," systematically listing the individuals from the official and private communities whom he will wish to invite to his home. Such a plan, once firmly thought out, can be adhered to more easily than one would think. In any event, it represents the best means yet devised to run one's own official entertainment schedule rather than be overrun by it.

The benefits of such a well-thought-through program go beyond representational objectives in the limited sense of that term. They offer an opportunity for expanding contacts. They provide an appropriate setting for maturing friendships. They often provide, too, the best of settings for quiet and unhurried conversations which lead in turn to increases in knowledge and mutual understanding. Under such circumstance much useful business can be done.

The official entertainment side of diplomacy, which has brought down so much opprobrium on the diplomat's head, has a serious and important purpose.

For a chief of mission, a key initial objective must be to help establish relationships with his host country's more senior officials and most influential groups. And once this is done, an important amount of continuing effort must be devoted to sustaining and developing these relationships. If he is resourceful, he will not let the process stop there, but will begin at once to plan ways to further widen and deepen his contacts.

He can next, to take a possible example, begin setting aside two evenings a week for quite a different program. On each evening he could invite two or three of his more junior embassy colleagues and their wives to the embassy residence for dinner—and each dinner would include an equal number of younger host-country nationals and their wives, whose names will have been supplied to the ambassador by the younger colleagues who are to be present at the same dinner. Thus over a period of time, all officers in all elements of the ambassador's embassy staff will have had an opportunity to nominate a host-country person with whom they do official business (or, if a private citizen, whom they value as a contact) for an embassy dinner invitation. If the dinners are kept small, as they should be, this can mean in a large embassy that two nights each week for many weeks and months will be tied up just on this program; and it can be a wearying effort when carried out in conjunction with all the other inevitable demands on an ambassador's evening schedules.

If the ambassador were otherwise engaged on these two evenings, the chances are these other activities would be just as much of a drain on his energies, without being either as useful or as interesting. For under the program of embassy dinners, he would not only be expanding his own contacts, he would also learn first hand the thinking of many host country persons whom he might otherwise never talk to; and he would be making clear his close association and admiration for the guests from his own staff, thus helping to strengthen their standing and effectiveness with their host country colleagues. And once such a program is completed, a valuable follow-up can be a similar effort, this time involving the embassy's secretarial and other support personnel and their host-country friends.

These simple examples are, of course, but a beginning. Sound planning will include quite different—or in some cases perhaps the same—programs aimed at university professors, undergraduate leaders, young politicians, writers, painters, musicians, sports figures, and so on into an endless list of fascinating possibilities and opportunities for both learning and influencing.

And now a few final points:

The first is that the whole social-representational side of diplomatic life is often excessively ostentatious and lavish. Hospitality must always be notably warm and generous, but luncheons, receptions and dinners surely can be so without taking on the opulence of a Roman banquet. Excessive lavishness is particularly distasteful in the case of embassies of poorer nations, many of whose people do not yet have some of life's barest necessities. But it is distasteful anywhere. Wastefulness and excess are hardly desirable "representative" qualities, even for nations who can better afford it.

There is often, of course, a large element of keeping up with the Joneses in all of this, especially on the part of smaller and poorer nations. But the richer nations are by no means immune to this same disease. They seem to forget that, in this area at least, they are the Joneses; and that instead of trying to keep up with themselves, they should be doing everyone a favor by setting more rational standards.

The second point is the reverse of the first. Sensible standards do not mean parsimonious ones. That surely is as unrepresentative of a reputable nation as is excess and waste. Guests must be received in a diplomat's home with a warm and sustained welcome, and the content of his table must be fully reflective of this.

Third, it is a mean and paltry business for nations to refuse adequate representational funds to their diplomats. It is shortsighted as well. Diplomats of all ranks, whose salaries are far from lavish, must dig deeply into their own limited pockets to carry on an important part of their work. And because there are obvious limits to what is in those pockets (unless independent wealth is there), some of that work is curtailed. It is, of course, illogical in the extreme to go to the far greater expense involved in recruiting and training and sending diplomatic officers overseas—and then deny them the relatively small added expenditures which allow them to carry out the job they were sent to do.

With respect to ambassadorial positions (and occasionally other very senior embassy positions just below that of the ambassador), the implications are even more pernicious. In the most expensive posts, where the incurring of very substantial representation costs is absolutely inevitable, these positions go only to the rich—rich careerists or rich outsiders. That only the rich can occupy certain high positions of government trust and responsibility is a reprehensible concept, thoroughly outmoded and repudiated in this day and age. Yet uninformed domestic political railing against "the whiskey fund" is cheap politics which, where successful, produces just this repugnant result.

As long as nations require diplomats, and as long as representational activities remain important in diplomatic work, the responsibility of those who control government expenditures is for something better than this. Clearly that responsibility is first to ensure that their diplomats' representational activities are effectively planned, and then to give them at least the minimum resources to get on with the job.

Fourth, there is no immutable law which says that even the more formal diplomatic functions have to be stuffy. With a little effort on the part of the host, decorum and enjoyment need never be mutually exclusive. And with a little imagination added, much can be done to relieve the "sameness" which burdens so much diplomatic entertaining. Not all dinners have to be black tie; barbecues and cookouts can often do the job and be more enjoyable in the process. And black-tie dinners themselves can often be enhanced by a basement game room with ping-pong and pool tables, shuffle and dart boards, and the like.

Unfortunately, sometimes an entertainment effort succeeds so well that a problem arises not generally encountered in private life. When the ranking guest in a private unofficial party is having such a good time that at the end of the evening he shows no sign of going home, it has no consequences for the other guests, who can take their leave whenever they wish. In diplomatic life, however, protocol requires that as a courtesy to the ranking guest, no one should leave before he does. When he overstays, it is perhaps a compliment to the occasion, but it is a compliment a thoughtful senior diplomat, when he is the ranking guest, will never pay. For it is also an imposition on fellow guests facing heavy schedules in the days and evenings to follow.

Fifth, and finally, the ability to give a good toast, when the occasion requires, is one of the minor but important skills which marks the professional diplomat. Toasts can be a useful tool in the diplomatic trade because they are often delivered before listeners of influence. Too often, however, the opportunity is wasted in graceful words that have no substance. Good toasts should be gracious, of course, and gracefully delivered, but they should also get across a useful point—one which the diplomat-speaker believes is important to convey at that particular time. They should also be brief.

As diplomats gain in experience, their words generally can be counted on to be graceful—but not always useful and not always brief. To ensure the presence of all three qualities, the wise diplomat knows that his words must be carefully prepared in advance. In this way only can he hope that they will constitute something more than pleasant but inconsequential grace notes on the diplomatic scene.

§

And now a concluding comment for this chapter which has focussed on a number of do's and don'ts respecting some of diplomacy's more traditional problem areas. A diplomat, and especially a chief of mission, must always remember that there is never one best way to do his job, that it can be done well in a number of different ways, and that a knowledge of its difficulties—not to mention the ethics of a decent person—requires him always to speak well of his predecessor and of his successor. To do otherwise is a mug's game, in which true professionals never indulge.

CHAPTER FOURTEEN
Problems New

IN ANY LISTING OF INSTITUTIONS which once played little or no role in the lives of American diplomats, but which now affect them to a striking degree, the Congress probably must be accorded the most prominent billing. There are, however, important rivals, the principal among them the United States Information Agency, the American foreign aid organization, and the Central Intelligence Agency. These significantly funded, broadly and professionally staffed new institutions (or their temporary predecessors) have played an increasingly important role in the United States foreign affairs effort since World War II.

Earlier was noted the basic incompatibility between a diplomat's instinct for discretion and a newsman's commitment to disclosure. But there is more to the story than that. In earlier times when governments were largely of an authoritarian character (or even when not, often tended to have, with the tacit consent of their citizens, a relatively free hand in foreign affairs), diplomats focused their attention almost exclusively on a very limited circle of influential host government officials. Public opinion could not, of course, be ignored altogether. For then as now, authoritarian regimes, even as generals in an army, could not completely disregard what their people were thinking. But the modern era, with its often embattled but resilient commitment to democracy, not to mention its fascination with public-opinion polls, presents an obviously enlarged challenge. The problem of "persuading a nation" enters the picture in a new and important way.

This is essentially the reason why many governments now have institutions like the U.S. Information Agency. These organizations vary considerably in character and operation. Some governments integrate them fully within their country's foreign-office structure. Some are separate from this structure, but work with it in a closely cooperative and coordinated relationship. Some believe their effectiveness lies in putting as much distance between themselves and their nation's foreign office as possible.

What each can do working abroad in any particular country will vary considerably in both scope and intensity, depending on the circumstances currently prevailing there. Some will recommend a high public profile for their ambassador, while in other circumstances they will recommend the opposite. Some will place particular reliance on Voice of America-type broadcasts sponsored by their headquarters back home. Some will tend to focus on working directly with the local press, with the purpose of getting a sympathetic objective presentation there of the information service's own nation's actions.

Others will seek these objectives more through the support of intellectual and cultural contacts between the people of the two nations involved. Here the emphasis is generally on exchange visits of private citizens and public officials, visiting-speakers programs, the establishment of library-reading centers and language-training facilities. Some information services pursue programs which embrace all these activities.

The purpose of all this is to bring to the citizens of a host country a better understanding of what the information service's country is all about, and what its people are really like. The ultimate objective is to achieve a sympathetic admiration for its character and its strength, and for what it stands for in the world, and finally, and most important, to obtain specific support for its international purposes.

This international advertising and public-relations business obviously has, because of its newness, much to learn. Three things about it, however, are certain.

The first is that no matter how unseemly all this appears to diplomats who cling to the more genteel standards of an earlier era, it is an effort which is here to stay. Blatant interference in the internal affairs of a host country must remain as repugnant today as it ever was, but information officers are going to be a permanent component of the more progressive and aggressive embassies. The second is that, young as this effort is, it already suffers from the problem of momentum, that is, from a tendency to continue to do things simply because it has fallen into the habit of doing them. The cost-benefit ratio of each activity should constantly be reexamined. The third is that while the search for ever-improving techniques must be a matter of continuing priority, ultimate success must depend in the end, as it does for its private domestic and commercial cousin, on the quality of the product it has to sell. If the product is a good one, however, its impact can be effectively enhanced by good advertising.

§

"Gentlemen do not read other gentlemen's mail" is a memorable comment attributed to Henry L. Stimson, the American Secretary of State in the years midway between World Wars I and II.

Unfortunately, historic distrust of the plans and purposes of others—at times bordering on the psychopathic—has been such that codebreaking and a wide range of other clandestine activities have been, since time immemorial, a regrettable but integral element in the nether reaches of international life. Occasional confirmation that the distrust has been well founded, together with the nearly universal belief that "if other nations use those tactics, so must we to protect ourselves," seem to have combined indelibly to inscribe them there.

Secretary Stimson's words have a special poignancy when it is remembered that they came but a few short years before activities of this kind, under the impetus of World War II, were to escalate to unprecedented levels of scope and intensity. Given the postwar penchant for big and complex organizations, not to mention its continuing suspicions and insecurities, it is not surprising that this escalation has continued into the modern era.

For the modern diplomat, then, it was not a new experience to find himself in a world where clandestine activities were operating both for and against his nation's interests. What was new was having so often to deal within his own government with the large and influential bureaucratic establishments which many nations had now organized to manage such activities.

Contrary to what is portrayed in novels and movies, the accomplishments of these massive new organizations in the intelligence field come largely from mundane sifting of thousands and thousands of small facts, often gained in the most mundane of ways—by reading, for example, with minute detail, all of a country's scientific journals, periodicals, and daily newspapers. It is grinding, cumulative, and unglamorous work, requiring special qualities of persistence and perception.

On the other hand, while clandestine activities play a far lesser role than is generally thought on the international scene, they are in fact ever present, and all nations must be on guard against them.

A diplomat should never, of course, engage in such activities himself. If he is an ambassador, however, he must ascertain what, if any, activities of this kind are being pursued by the intelligence bureaucracy of his own country in the area where he is serving. He must ensure that these remain within the bounds of internationally unacknowledged, but generally accepted, perimeters for such matters. Most important, he should ensure that the potential benefits from any particular activity are not clearly outweighed by the potential damage that would flow from their disclosure. He should take a particularly jaundiced look at the latter.

A contrary stance, which some senior diplomats have found appealing, is to want to know nothing at all of such activities unless they are about to be exposed—in which case, to quote one practitioner of this view, he "would appreciate twenty minutes' advance notice."

This has the obvious advantage of leaving a diplomat unassociated with such activities, and in a position to state publicly, after disclosure, that he knew nothing of them. But in most situations, it is also a cop-out. Much as he should prefer a world in which such things are not part of the international scene, as long as they do go on he cannot prevent their abuse with his head in the sand.

The large and relatively new bureaucracies at home which are responsible for such activities must be kept under firm control of other governmental elements. This means not only of the president or prime minister and state departments or foreign offices, but also of fully informed parliamentary watchdog committees. In a dangerous world, these organizations have performed important services to their countries. And because of the dangers of that world, it is not surprising that they pursue their work with energy and zeal. It is because of this very zeal and commitment, however, that it is especially important that they never are placed in the position of having to be the final arbiters of the limits of their own activities.

§

The world today is made up of a few rich peoples and a great many who are very poor. Extremes of this kind cannot prevail indefinitely. As President Kennedy said in his inaugural address: "If a free society cannot help the many who are poor, it cannot save the few who are rich."

Sacrifice and determination in the developing countries and a sense of fairness and self-interest in their more economically developed neighbors have combined to produce something new in the world: foreign-aid efforts, noncolonial in character, and unprecedented in scope. Despite its chilling inadequacies (some developed nations spend more on lipstick than they do on foreign aid), this combined effort of rich and poor to elevate the human condition remains a credit in a world of many debits.

From its start it has been a controversial effort, however, and one which has suffered considerably from the oversimplification of the debate which has surrounded it. The following exchange, which took place a number of years ago, after several days of testimony before a congressional appropriations committee, has an all too familiar ring:

"The Chairman: To me this [foreign aid] program is the silliest thing ever conceived by the mind of man.

"Witness: Rather than being one of the silliest things ever conceived by the mind of man . . .

"The Chairman (interrupting): That is my opinion and you could not change my mind if you took the difference between your age and my age and spent all that time trying.

"Witness: I have a suspicion that I am not going to change your mind.

"The Chairman: Don't be suspicious. I give you positive assurance that you are not going to.

"Witness: I accept that positive assurance. I suspect that history will one day judge this program as one of the . . .

"The Chairman (interrupting): Biggest flops?

"Witness (continuing): . . . finer things conceived by the mind of a nation, not only because it served that nation's own self-interest, but because it brought inestimable good and progress in the world which is, after all, one of the fundamental purposes of that nation."

As one of the participants in that exchange, I am partial to the words of the witness. It is the kind of oversimplified dialogue on both sides, however, which inhibits rather than encourages understanding.

Talk of "Operation Rat Hole," of "charity begins at home," and of the "ingratitude of aid recipients" is equally off the point. Compared, for example, to the waste and inefficiency that takes place daily in a war effort—and in many peacetime military establishments as well—the level of waste and inefficiency in economic assistance programs is relatively small. Comparisons of this kind aside, it is still unfortunately true that there has been more waste and inefficiency than anyone would like. But, given both the newness and scale of the effort, the report card on this point is not too bad a one.

As for charity beginning at home: this program is not charity. It is designed to help peoples who are prepared to help themselves. Even if it were charity, there is no great principle that says that charity must end where it begins. As for gratitude: only the most naïve ever considered this to be the objective.

The true objective is a mix of altruism and self-interest. Decent people have always felt an obligation to help persons less fortunate than themselves. And this is particularly true when they are dealing with persons who have been disadvantaged by factors beyond their control. A foreign economic aid program is, in part, simply a projection of this feeling onto the international scene.

And because of this, these congressionally beleaguered programs are never quite as totally devoid of domestic political support as is sometimes asserted. While these programs tend to have great difficulty in getting necessary support in the countries which provide aid, elected officials who, too callously, ignore their altruistic function will hear from church groups and other similarly motivated organizations and individuals.

These programs have a coldly calculated element of self-interest as well. In relative and in absolute terms, the bulk of the world's people are not just a little poor, they are terribly poor. Illiteracy, disease, malnutrition continue to plague them to a degree still not fully comprehended in the developed world. And what is new, of course, is that people suffering from these age-old scourges have learned through the communications explosion that this does not have to be, that elsewhere people have found the key to a better life.

The result is an insatiable, militant, and explosive demand for this better life—for themselves if possible, for their children at whatever cost. The problem is compounded by a lack of appreciation of the complexity and difficulty of developing both the human skills and the economic base essential for this better life. Impatience, not understanding, prevails; and this perhaps as much as any other factor is why the modern world is such a turbulent, volatile, explosive, and dangerous place. As long as this tension remains the prospects for peace are reduced.

No economic aid program can diminish these tensions by in effect handing over a developed economy to a developing country. Nor is that necessary. What is essential, however, is a sense on the part of developing peoples that they are making significant progress toward a better life.

To achieve this sense of progress so critical to stability and world order, to enable nations through their own efforts to move to this better life, there is often a desperate need for outside capital, technical skills, and training which are simply not available through the world's more normal channels and facilities. Providing these otherwise un-available essentials is one of the most important things that a well-designed aid program is all about.

A fundamental purpose of foreign economic assistance, inherent in what has just been said, is to contribute in important ways to the increase in world productivity. Here again the program is in the interest of the rich as well as the poor. In a world which threatens future shortages in food and other necessities of life, all of us can be its beneficiaries.

Foreign-aid programs will not accomplish any of their objectives if diplomats, and all others concerned with these objectives, fail to keep in mind the key lessons which have clearly emerged from our historically brief, but now rather extensive, experience with them.

Perhaps most important, no economic assistance program will be anything but a waste of money unless there is a bona fide commitment on the part of the aid-receiving country to a matching self-help effort. Otherwise, aid is in fact perverted into handouts which eventually disappear into the sand.

Aid officials in an embassy should never be pressured by their diplomatic colleagues to agree to finance or otherwise participate in an economically unsound project. Diplomats, misconceiving assistance resources as a sort of diplomatic slush fund, can occasionally fall into this error. They do so in response to the urgings of host country officials who, in turn, are responding to domestic political pressures. However, if a host country ends up burdened by an unsound project, its officials, after praising the aid donor for a few weeks, will, as flaws become apparent, become resentful and continue so for years to come. Bad projects in the long run are the worst kind of diplomacy.

An aid effort must also be selective. Working in a large number of areas within a developing country inevitably means that an aid program is spread too thin. Granted that the need for assistance is wide-ranging and the pressure from developing nations often intense, experience has shown that concentration behind a relatively few activities will, in the end, produce the most impressive and useful results.

Aid efforts must be designed for breakthroughs. Aid programs must guard against simply grafting themselves onto what is happening anyway, and taking false satisfaction from the progress which follows. The combination of intelligent people in a developing country and a felt need for progress in a specific area (say, for example, in public administration) will result over a twenty-year period in considerable progress in that area. Taxpayers in an aid-giving country are being cheated by their aid officials if aid resources lead only to a slightly better performance accomplished in a somewhat briefer time, say, sixteen or eighteen years rather than twenty. That is not what an aid program is for. If it cannot achieve in six or eight years what would otherwise take twenty, it should stay out of that area.

Like so many other things in government, aid programs suffer from the problem of momentum. If aid officials do not take care, they will find that the design of their programs takes on a certain sameness around the developing world, despite the variety of situations with which they are contending, simply because this is the way they have fallen into the habit of doing things. Aid officials also have a tendency to stay with an unsuccessful project too long. Always beware of the official who reports in connection with a particular project, not hitherto successful, that "just last week" or last month or whatever, a favorable development occurred which will transform this sick project into the healthy one it was intended to be. If it is an unsuccessful project, and has been for some time, it is time to cut one's losses and cancel it out.

There is also a tendency to stay with successful projects and programs too long. Nations graduate from a need for foreign economic assistance, not when they have been developed economically, or even very nearly so. They should graduate when they reach what economists term "the point of self-sustaining growth." Put another way, this means that foreign economic aid should cease when a developing country's economy has reached the point where its development effort is bankable. It can now fund its outside financial and other development needs through the more customary world channels.

Aid personnel, pleased by what a program has achieved, and always aware of what remains to be accomplished, are inclined to opt for "one more year." This should almost always be resisted. Although foreign-aid programs play a critical role at the start, in the end even the largest represent but a minuscule portion of the resources any developing country needs. They prime the pump in the early and crucial days, but in the end they should be dwarfed by the role of conventional foreign investment and lending resources from abroad, and especially by the massive commitment of human and economic resources of the developing country itself. It is as important to the taxpaying interests of a donor country to know when to end a program as it is, from the point of view of its other interests, to know when it should begin.

From a personnel organizational point of view, aid agencies do not need the same type of structure required by their sister organizations in the foreign affairs community. These other organizations recruit primarily in the most junior ranks, themselves providing the experience and training needed, and generally retain their personnel through a lifetime career. A diplomat learns his trade from his own organization. The wide range, however, of expertise that aid agencies require—in agriculture, road building, public administration, health, financial management, dam building, factory management, or whatever—cannot be taught "in house." These must be learned and practiced extensively elsewhere before they can be of any value to an aid agency. An aid organization should, in marked contrast with its sister agencies, be built on lateral entry and temporary appointments.

A small cadre of permanent career professionals should be on hand to plan and to manage the agency's activities; the bulk of the organization should be experts and specialists brought in on contract for two- or four-year stints only. The agency can, because of the fascinating assignments it has to offer, recruit outstanding talent from the private sector, from universities, and from other government agencies. By relying on contracts, it can at the same time avoid saddling itself indefinitely with talent no longer needed.

Massive military-assistance efforts have been of marked importance, too, in the post-World War II era. These also have played a critical role in the effort to build stability in a volatile world. They have been used to prevent power imbalances, and to head off the aggressions such imbalances almost inevitably invite.

It is unfortunate that resources devoted to this type of aid could not have been assigned instead to economic nation building, but that simply has not been practical in the world as it is. On the other hand, military-assistance programs, to the extent they have contributed to the peace, also have contributed to nation building, for peace is one of nation building's obvious essentials. Moreover, by funding a significant portion of a developing country's needs in the defense field, they serve to release a larger portion of its scarce resources for economic development.

Self-help, political pressures for unwise expenditures, selectivity, all the problems of momentum, including a reluctance toward graduation, affect military assistance just as they affect economic assistance.

The most difficult problem in military assistance, however, is the ascertaining of a specific developing country's true defense needs. Military authorities are, by instinct, cautious. And the instinct to be safe rarely leads to underestimation of needs by the military authorities of either the aid-receiving or the aid-extending nation. When the two work together the bill can come very high, indeed.

§

Parliamentary diplomacy is still in its embryonic stages. The weaknesses of the old League of Nations and the present United Nations have made many observers more conscious of its flaws than of its promise.

In parliamentary diplomacy, the diplomat must draw on all the skills required for bilateral diplomacy, and encounter all of bilateral diplomacy's frustrations. He must master the traditional parliamentary skills and suffer the classic frustrations of all parliamentary bodies. The latter are not made easier to bear by the knowledge that they are inflicted upon him by a weak and often ineffectual institution.

The flaws of parliamentary diplomacy, as exemplified by the United Nations, are so well known that they scarcely need detailing here. What is unfortunate, however, is that the United Nations lacks an historic record of accomplishment of sufficient duration to allow for some of its shortcomings, serious as they are, to be viewed in a fairer perspective. For example, if the United States Congress were daily subject to the same instant judgments so often applied to the United Nations, it would probably come away with almost as bad marks. Surely the logrolling, the obstructionism, the posturing for home consumption, the long-winded speeches, and other nonadmirable habits are on display there each day as well.

Americans have learned over the course of two hundred years, however, that their congressional system works, and because they know it works, they don't find themselves judging it each day. With all its flaws and foolishness, it has proven itself over the years to be an invaluable institution. The U.N. does not have the luxury of a similar perspective in which to view its shortcomings.

The Congress, of course, has authority which the U.N. does not have. In fact, it is not realistic to expect the United Nations to gain significantly in authority as long as world circumstances remain as they are. But even so, the world is better off with it than without it. It has, in its relatively short existence, already made contributions of consequence to the cause of peace. And while it is not now, nor likely to become, a substitute for bilateral diplomacy, it carries a potential, frail but as promising as any we have, for the strengthening of the rule of law in international dealings. For this reason alone, flaws notwithstanding, it merits the interest and support of all diplomats.

§

Another striking new dimension recently added to diplomatic life has been the constant overseas travel of high-level figures who formerly departed their capitals for such purposes only on the rarest of occasions. Almost commonplace now, in the life of diplomats, is the arrival on the scene of their president, secretary of state, or other cabinet ministers and senators and congressmen; not to mention a whole host of lesser government officials. In fact, it is so common that it becomes difficult to recall how relatively new this practice is.

Up to World War II, and for a few years immediately thereafter, hardly any of this went on. Travel facilities, as they then existed, made it too costly of the travelers' time. Diplomats were by and large the only officials of their country whom host-country officials ever saw. Now that almost every nook and cranny of the earth is quickly reachable, all this has, of course, radically changed. And what is surely clear is that this is not going to change back. The days of a diplomat's isolation, in this particular sense, are over forever.

Some diplomats resent this. They complain about the burdens of hotel keeping and of running a visitors' bureau. And some, one suspects, are concerned about being upstaged.

The era of travel becomes a clear plus for them nonetheless. The arrival of a president, secretary of state, or other high official on the scene, if accompanied by a normal show of confidence and support, enhances the standing of the resident diplomat, not the contrary. And nothing is more calculated to advance a diplomat's objectives than having host-country officials hear of them directly from such senior figures. Nothing is more calculated to get the attention of both the host country and of high-level visitors focused on bilateral relationships. And when high-level visitors are on the scene, their diplomats can expect to get far more of their time and attention than when the venue is reversed and the diplomats are home on consultations.

The stream of lower-level visitors can, of course, constitute a burden on the time and other resources of the embassy. But the compensations are very great. They can bring information and expertise which is cumulatively invaluable to the embassy's operations. And these visits lead almost invariably to more effective working relationships between the embassy and the visitors after they have returned home.

In the relatively rare cases where the burden of this stream of lower-level visitors becomes so disruptive as temporarily to outweigh its benefits, the ambassador has the clear authority to shut off the flow; and he should, of course, have no hesitation in doing so.

CHAPTER FIFTEEN

The Diplomat and Congress

LOOKING BACK ON THE BEGINNINGS of what was to be a notable forty-year career of diplomatic service, Charles E. "Chip" Bohlen has written that the "workload at State was light and there were few crises to worry about." He added, "Virtually the only contact with the Congress was the annual review of the budget.... Regular closed-door hearings and the constant interchange of views which are now such a ... part of the relations of State and the Congress were unknown in 1929." Of all the changed circumstances with which a modern American diplomat must contend, none has become more important than the vastly expanded interest, and role, of the Congress in foreign affairs.

§

In the early days of the republic, George Washington, as its first president, became involved in negotiating a treaty with the Indians. Mindful that the Constitution required that a treaty be made "with the advice and consent of the Senate," he journeyed one day to the Congress to consult about the proposed treaty with the members of the Senate, who were at that time only slightly more in total number than the present Senate Foreign Relations Committee, and considerably smaller in number than the present House Foreign Affairs Committee. Apparently, the President received more advice than he had bargained for, and much of it not particularly to his liking.

Legend reports his irritation, his abrupt departure from the Senate, and his emphatically expressed determination never to go there again.

He never did. And some might argue that this episode marked the beginnings of the difficulties between the American Congress and the executive in the field of foreign affairs.

Actually their roots predate this incident and lie in the wording of the Constitution itself. That document, so admirable in so many respects, causes much difficulty in this area. It does so by assigning certain clear foreign-policy powers to Congress as a whole, namely, to declare war, to regulate foreign commerce, to control appropriations—and to the Senate alone to authorize the ratification of treaties and to confirm presidential ambassadorial nominations. At the same time, it assigns other, roughly equal, powers to the executive, namely, to send and to receive ambassadors, to negotiate treaties, and to command the armed forces. Even more significant, with respect to many other powers, it remains totally silent.

Thus the Constitution, in the notable phrase of Professor Edward S. Corwin, is for the executive and legislative branches of this American government "an invitation to struggle for the privilege of directing American foreign policy." The issue that is joined does not relate to who carries out foreign policy. That responsibility clearly belongs to the executive branch. The issue is over who controls the direction and content of that policy.

While the number of specific powers assigned to the Congress exceed those assigned to the President, it is generally assumed that the founding fathers intended that the President have the stronger role. Whether or not an accurate assumption, this has from the beginning been the practical necessity and the historic result. But while the executive has dominated through the years, the Congress has always retained very substantial power to influence foreign policy, whenever it chose to exercise that influence.

A significant fact is, however, that Congress for many years chose not to use that power or rather to do it spasmodically. In a sense it abdicated the struggle of which Professor Corwin speaks. The reason is clear enough; its focus of interest was elsewhere.

For many years the congressional focus was inward—on the westward expansion of the country, on the economic crises that periodically wracked it, on the issues which were to lead eventually to civil war. It pretty much left the President and the State Department alone in the foreign-policy field.

There were important exceptions, of course. The Senate failed through the years with disquieting regularity to consent to the ratification of a number of important treaties, and did so in connection with others only after some strenuous battles. The War of 1812 and the Spanish-American War are generally considered to be the result of congressional rather than executive foreign policy. Certainly the Congress had a large hand in them.

There are other examples, too, but by and large for nearly the first 150 years following the adoption of the Constitution, the field was left to the executive branch.

This does not mean that there was not throughout our history continual contact on this subject, between the executive and the Congress. The first permanent committee the Congress established was the Senate Foreign Relations Committee, and this naturally kept a monitoring eye on matters in this area.

When President Washington made his historic exit from the Senate, someone had to take up where he left off. The task fell to Thomas Jefferson, the first secretary of state, as it has fallen on every succeeding secretary of state.

The custom almost immediately developed for each secretary of state to designate a senior official on his staff to assist him in this task. The work was such that it rarely involved the rank and file of the department, as the young Chip Bohlen was to discover so many years later. In fact, it was sufficiently light that for many years the senior official responsible for this function could handle it in addition to other duties. He was aided by the fact that, appropriations matters aside, the State Department traditionally dealt primarily with one committee—the Foreign Relations Commiteee—in one body—the Senate—and on many matters with only one man, the chairman of that committee.

It is often said that the Senate's rejection of the Versailles Treaty following World War I marked the beginning of the end of the long period of relative congressional indifference to foreign-policy matters. Nevertheless, for fifteen years following that struggle, the Congress again lapsed into relative disinterest. A resurgence of interest came with the passage of the reciprocal trade legislation—involving the regulation of foreign commerce, a specific congressional power—in the early 1930's, and then with the gathering of the war clouds in Europe which presaged the coming of World War II.

It was at that point that members of Congress realized, once and for all, that what was happening beyond the seas was as important to them, and to their constituents, as any of their domestic concerns. Confirmed in this belief by the events of World War II, and what has happened since, they are not likely to lose interest again for years to come.

Since the mid- and late 1930's, therefore, the Congress has been, in effect, battling itself back into the foreign-policy act. Its members have been doing so, however, under very serious disadvantages.

For many years the field had been left to the executive, which had fallen into deeply ingrained habits of handling these matters with a minimum of congressional interference. Habits of this kind become difficult to change.

In addition, it is the President, not the Congress, who sends ambassadors and receives them, who has the key information, who has the initiative, who commands the Armed Forces, who is one man in charge of his branch of government, not 535 persons struggling among themselves to control theirs. Moreover, it is to the President rather than to members of Congress, either collectively or singularly, that the American people traditionally turn for their basic foreign-policy leadership.

And if these obstacles were not enough, congressional efforts to play an increasingly key role were additionally handicapped by the fact that this desire coincided with the enormous increase in the complexity and range of American foreign interests and with the consequent proliferation of foreign-affairs interests and objectives throughout the executive branch.

The point of mentioning it again now is that once this proliferation began in the executive branch it was gradually duplicated in the Congress. It was soon not just the Senate Foreign Relations Committee which had a direct interest in such matters. As the Agriculture Department became involved in foreign policy, so did the Senate Agriculture Committee; as the Treasury Department's interests increased, so did the Senate Finance Committee's; and so on until almost every Senate committee had become involved. And because almost everything in foreign policy began, it seemed, soon to involve money, the House of Representatives also became a full participant in this process. Not just its Foreign Affairs Committee, but soon almost all of its committees also had legitimate and important interests in overseas developments and ties. We have seen what difficulties this proliferation caused within the executive branch. It is not difficult to imagine the complicating impact these comparable developments had on Congress's operations as well.

In addition, the Congress, unlike the executive, has no single leader, and nothing approaching an overall National Security Committee to play a counterpart role to the executive's National Security Council. The result is somewhat as though the executive branch were trying to operate with a series of more or less equal departments, but without a president or without any coordinating machinery—not once but twice over, because the Congress duplicates itself in both bodies.

When Congress passes a law in the foreign-affairs area, it has in effect made a coordinated decision and this decision is controlling on the executive. But a great deal is done by the executive in the foreign-affairs field, in contrast with the domestic front, which does not rely on, and generally is not controlled by, specific legislative action.

Nevertheless, congressional views can be critically important, even where the legislative process is not. But what are Congress's views? Surely they are as varied across the spectrum of Congress as they are initially across the executive-branch spectrum. The difference is that the executive has a president who with his supporting machinery can reach a conclusion. Congress often cannot make up its mind in such a definitive way. Often Congress ends, as it begins, with many viewpoints—with seriously adverse consequences on its influence.

Actually, the problems of proliferation were camouflaged for a time by a quirk of historical circumstance at both ends of Pennsylvania Avenue. During the very years that interest in foreign policy was spreading most rapidly throughout the Congress, the Foreign Relations Committee in the Senate happened to be led, *seriatim*, by Senators Connally, Vandenberg, and George. Because of their unique personal standing in the Congress as a whole, their personal prestige and influence, these men were able to continue to constitute in their persons a natural focal point with which the State Department could continue to deal. They could be extremely tough negotiators, but, once convinced, they were generally able to bring the Congress with them.

At the other end of the avenue, the State Department was led similarly during the latter portion of this period by three unusually strong secretaries: General George Marshall, Dean Acheson, and John Foster Dulles. Formidable figures in their own right and with the unfaltering support of their presidents, these men represented in their persons a continuing focal point which, during the period of their incumbencies, suppressed from general view the degree to which the forces of proliferation were already at work in the executive branch.

For a little time more the executive-congressional relationship seemed to go on as it always had—that is, guided by, and conducted within, the simple dual-pole system that had operated for so many years, with the chairman of the Senate Foreign Relations Committee acting as the principal agent of the Congress and the Secretary of State playing a similar role for the executive.

Not until these unique figures had passed from the scene was it possible to sense just how much the proliferation of interest, and the determination to carve out myriad separate roles, had spread at both ends of the avenue. The implications within the executive branch have been examined earlier. With respect to the Congress, it has meant that the State Department, while still giving priority to the Senate Foreign Relations Committee and the House Foreign Affairs Committee, must deal now with all the Congress, committee by committee, group by group, individual by individual.

It is an endless task, one certainly that the assistant secretary charged with directing this, long since a full-time responsibility, cannot hope, with his own small staff, to fulfill. For this reason, as the years have gone on, more and more of the department's diplomatic personnel, from the most senior to the most junior, have become involved in the testimony, briefings, and other contacts which now make up the massive intercourse which daily takes place between the State Department and the Congress. The focus of these contacts is in Washington, but with the advent of congressional travel abroad, a surprising amount of it takes place in embassies as well.

All this represents for the modern diplomat a major added ingredient to his job. For some time he has been required to understand foreign parliaments, but he has, until relatively recently, been separated from direct involvement in the tumult and turmoil of his own. And the job of persuading his Congress to a particular action, or to support a particular policy, is an almost entirely new responsibility. In the past, this was taken on, when necessary, by the relatively few specialists, or very senior officers, and was not his concern.

It is fashionable in the press and elsewhere to criticize congressional travel as junkets, boondoggling, and a waste of taxpayers' money. Congressmen themselves are aware of these charges and sometimes are reluctant to travel because of them. Despite the occasional traveler who is, in fact, a boondoggling, junketeering waster of the taxpayers' money, this is a valuable activity much in the national interest. Regardless of the disadvantages the Congress must struggle against, it has a major influence and role in American foreign policy and nothing can better prepare its members for that role than firsthand knowledge gained at the scene of the problems with which they must deal.

Embassies should especially welcome congressional visitors. Washington is the congressman's home turf, and his dealings with American diplomats have a different chemistry there than they do abroad. In Washington, the diplomat, figuratively, and often quite literally, looks up at a raised horseshoe of congressional interrogators. Abroad, the relationship alters. The congressman does not have to take an instant formal position on all that is said. He has come to learn, and it is the diplomat who knows. The good ones come as students with the raised-dais atmosphere totally absent. Temporarily separated from many of the burdens that harass them in Washington, they can devote themselves exclusively to the subject at hand as they often cannot at home. And while members of Congress rarely single out for special praise American diplomats they have first encountered in Washington, time and again they will speak well of a diplomatic official they have met abroad.

There is still another benefit to be gathered from congressional visits. While it is the embassy, not members of Congress, which conducts the nation's business abroad, legislators have a much greater sense of being on the same team when they are overseas together than they do in the atmosphere of the legislative-executive rivalry at home. As a result, they have proven time and again to be of invaluable help, in their talks with host country officials, in underscoring previously expressed embassy viewpoints and supporting embassy objectives. Occasionally, their conduct can be unhelpful, but this is relatively rare. Taken in the balance, the pluses of congressional travel outweigh the minuses by a convincing margin.

Unfortunately if a member of Congress were asked to sum up in one word his feelings on his foreign-policy role, that word would be "frustration." The source of this frustration is, of course, in part the executive. But in large part it lies closer to home. Outsiders forget sometimes how intensely competitive Congress is within itself.

If a member wishes to promote a congressionally sponsored initiative in the foreign-affairs area, his first and often most difficult hurdles will come, not from the executive, but from the opposition or inertia of his own colleagues, and from the jurisdictional and personal rivalries and combativeness which abound in both bodies. And this will be so regardless of whether the executive favors or opposes the particular initiative in question. The great bulk of congressional initiatives are generally smothered in this way, and the fact that many of them deserve to be does not lessen the feeling of frustration on the part of their sponsor. And occasionally, an initiative which is suppressed in this way deserves a better fate.

If, by the exercise of very considerable legislative skill, a member surmounts the odds against him and secures favorable action in his own chamber, he has still to get his idea approved by the other body—which can also be a competitive, combative experience, and a source of further frustration, again whether or not the executive has a view for or against.

The result is that it often seems to the legislator that the many conflicting ideas at loose in the Congress present for the executive what is in effect a menu, from which it can choose more or less what it likes. Relatively few such ideas reach the point of having such overwhelming congressional support that they become musts which the executive must accept. As for the others, the executive, it seems, simply pursues the ones it approves, and ignores the ones it does not. It is a frustrating situation, indeed, for those members who would like to guide the executive, rather than simply to offer a range of choices.

And finally if merit, legislative skill, and fortuitous circumstances combine to produce favorable action in both houses, it often seems to the frustrated sponsor that the executive branch, accustomed to going its own way for so many years in the foreign-affairs field, will still find a way to circumvent congressional wishes.

The frustration does not simply run one way. President Kennedy is reported to have said that when he was in Congress, he did not think it had much influence, and it was not until he got to the other end of Pennsylvania Avenue that he fully appreciated how much influence and power it truly had. In any event, from the vantage point of the executive, Congress has impressive power in the foreign-affairs field, regardless of many of its members' conclusions to the contrary.

The frustration comes for the executive, and for its diplomats, because it so often seems that congressional force is used for negative and disruptive purposes. As the member of Congress is frustrated by his seeming lack of influence, so the diplomat feels put upon by what seems to him a much too frequent undermining by the Congress of the critical undertakings in which he is engaged.

A certain amount of mutual frustration is not, of course, a serious matter. The founding fathers built it into most constitutional relationships, and it would be unnatural if it were ever totally absent. To use Secretary Acheson's phrase, the relations between the Congress and the executive "were not designed to be restful."

Congress, however, cannot expect to take over in the foreign-affairs area. History, and the logic of the very different circumstances under which the two branches must operate, not to mention the general expectations of the people, clearly point to the President's continued leadership in this field.

But the importance of Congress, and its deep involvement, in foreign affairs is also here to stay. There is no turning back. And while a certain amount of consequent frustration is natural and inevitable, this can, if it is allowed to get out of hand, have disastrous consequences on the strength and stability of the nation's foreign policy. As the years go on, better ways must be found to clarify the roles of these two great branches of government. And important efforts, too, must be made to ensure that they complement one another more, and frustrate each other somewhat less. It is an unfolding process in which many answers are left for the future.

§

It is a process, however, in which certain truths have already emerged. It is clear, for example, that it has now become as important for the diplomat to understand his own Congress as it has traditionally been for him to understand the working and viewpoints of foreign parliaments—and it remains a source of amazement that some diplomats can be so perceptive about the latter and so unperceptive about their own.

It is also clear that modern American diplomats cannot avoid altogether being pulled into the hurly-burly of active and often combative executive-congressional relationships, and through this to some degree into the nation's domestic and partisan political processes. The President cannot be brought before the Congress on foreign policy matters, but the diplomat as the President's agent can. His first loyalty is to the chief executive, and this can, on occasion, in a directly personal sense, result in congressional antagonism which may subsequently encumber his career.

This is a risk the diplomat can never eliminate altogether. He can limit it considerably, however, if he zealously avoids ever being "cute" in his dealings with Congress. Such dealings almost always stand revealed, and the consequences to the perpetrator can be disastrous and lasting. He must tell the truth. Discretion permits him not to tell all he knows, but what is said must be straightforward and accurate, and if something is withheld, it must be done in a way so as not to mislead.

In talking to members, he must also guard against the tendency to tailor what is said to what are known to be his listeners' views and inclinations. When I first became active in the State Department's congressional liaison activities, Senator Styles Bridges and the young Senator Hubert Humphrey represented two poles of conservative-liberal thinking in the Senate. I found it a useful device as I was briefing either on a particular subject to make certain that I was using the same words I would use with the other. That can burden an individual interview, but it is as good a device as I know to strengthen long-time credibility and trust.

No matter how able the American diplomat becomes in this overall field, however, he will learn that just as the relations between nations are no tea party, neither are they between the executive and legislative branches of his own government. The legislative is generally in an aggressive, predatory mood, belatedly determined to expand its role in the foreign-affairs field. On the other hand, the diplomats will find that all presidents they serve, no matter how different in other respects, are militantly determined to leave the powers of their office intact for their successors—and this specifically includes leaving the influence of the presidency undiminished in the foreign-affairs area.

The diplomat who operates on the assumption that he knows more about a subject than the member of Congress he is briefing, or before whom he is testifying, is often in for a shock. Unlike diplomats, members of Congress do not inevitably rotate to a new job every few years. As a result, a member who has been in the Congress for a long time, and who has taken a long-time interest in a particular foreign-policy subject, may well know considerably more about it than the diplomat-witness appearing before him. The lesson of this, of course, is never, ever, to deal with members of Congress without having done your homework.

The Foreign Affairs and Foreign Relations Committees of the House and Senate respectively often feel themselves at a disadvantage in passing judgment on the work of the State Department, when they are largely dependent, in the reaching of that judgment, on the information being supplied to them by the department itself.

As a result, diplomats will see these two committees constantly seeking supplementary and independent sources of information and opinion. One solution, pursued from time to time, is the expansion of the committees' professional staffs. This can turn into an endless process, and what the nation's interest does not need is the building of a large and competing new bureaucracy in the foreign-affairs business.

Other alternative sources the members seek to exploit include the press, and the expertise lodged on university campuses, and the General Accounting Office, a congressional instrumentality used increasingly to audit policy rather than just accounts. Still another important source the committees cultivate and encourage to be forthcoming are the executive's other departments and agencies actively engaged in foreign affairs.

The attitude of the Senate Foreign Relations Committee and the House Foreign Affairs Committee toward these other government departments and agencies is significant, however. They are quite prepared to use them, as a cross check for both information and viewpoint, in their efforts to judge the work of the State Department. They are strongly opposed, on the other hand, to these other departments' being allowed to make inroads on the State Department's influence and authority. Here, of course, there is an important consideration of self-interest. The State Department is "their" department. The other departments are basically oriented to other committees of the Congress. To the extent, therefore, there is a dispersion of influence and authority from State to these other institutions in the executive, a similar trend, contrary to the interests of these parent committees in the House and Senate, is likely to ensue on Capitol Hill. As a result, diplomats can generally count on "their" two committees to play a key role through the years as critical, but protective, parents.

§

As it is in the case of all executive branch departments, the passage of the State Department's annual budget appropriation is of key importance to all its personnel. The effort to obtain the appropriation each year, however, tends to be a job for specialists in the department rather than for the rank and file of its members. It is a highly specialized task, largely involving technical witnesses and budget experts, rather than the population of the department as a whole.

All diplomats would do well to understand the appropriations process better, however, and especially to have a clearer picture of where the main difficulty lies. The general impression is that the often severe and unwarranted budget stringencies which are inflicted upon the State Department are primarily the result of shortsighted congressional attitudes. Often, it is not what happens in that forum which is the problem. It is what happens on the way to the forum which causes the trouble. For example, in the years when I was responsible for the department's budget, while congressional attitudes were responsible for some key shortages—notably in official entertainment allowances—the bulk of the problem lay with the government's central Budget Bureau.

Despite its occasionally caustic oratory, it was a little-recognized fact that the Congress quietly appropriated almost everything the department asked for. The crippling cuts were imposed ahead of time by the Executive Budget Bureau, through its inhibiting what the department was allowed to request. Despite the fact that the State Department's budget was lower than any other department's in the executive branch, it seemed (in an admittedly not altogether objective view) to be subject to a level of Executive Budget Bureau scrutiny which many other departments, with powerful lobbies behind them, appeared to escape.

§

Far more crucial in many instances than the legislative relationships for the diplomat is the consultative one. The objective here is to ascertain congressional attitudes on foreign-policy developments, and to ensure that these attitudes are taken into account as policy is developed by the State Department and the executive branch as a whole. The task, of course, is a difficult one, for Congress does not speak with one voice, and it often confronts the executive with a gamut of widely diverse opinions.

The consultative process is not simply for ascertaining attitudes; it is for conditioning them, as well. This involves keeping the Congress informed of all important foreign policy developments, actual and anticipated, and explaining the State Department judgment as to the true factors involved. It entails explaining their significance, and what in the department's judgment should be done about them. The purpose is to ensure that as the executive moves to meet these developments, the necessary congressional support will be forthcoming.

This effort must lie at the heart of the congressional liaison program, and the reason is simple enough. For despite constitutional ambiguities, the basic fact is that no policy is going to be successful if anything like 51 per cent of the Congress is mobilized against it. This is true regardless of whether legislative action is required or not.

Put another way, for a policy to succeed, it does not, unless legislation is directly involved, require having 51 per cent of the Congress mobilized for it. But it cannot have over half the Congress organized against it. If it does, it will fail no matter how sound it may intrinsically be, because it simply won't be credible.

Opposition to a policy, if it is strongly felt and well organized, can have a serious impact, even if it emanates from considerably fewer than 51 per cent of the Congress's total membership. The opposition to the Vietnam War policy is a case in point. In the end, the percentage of opposition was very high, but for several critically important earlier years, when the opposition ran only between 25 and 30 per cent of the Senate and 12 and 15 per cent of the House, it managed to be of great importance, nevertheless. (Its impact was abetted by the fact that in the Senate this opposition was strategically centered in that body's leadership, and in its Foreign Relations Committee.)

To carry out an effective consultation program, it has become necessary to mobilize a large portion of the human resources of the State Department. From the Secretary on down, a vast number of departmental officials must of necessity spend long hours diverted from their other duties, consulting with, and explaining to, the Congress.

In this process of seeking congressional support, the Department of State, unlike many other departments, does not, as previously noted, have the support of a constituency of its own in the body politic. In this respect, it is unlike, for example, the Defense Department with its veterans' groups, the Agriculture Department with its farm groups, the Commerce Department with its business groups, and the Labor Department with its unions. The State Department without the ability to mobilize such forces on behalf of its viewpoints must rely entirely on its persuasive powers and on the logic of its position.

On the whole, this process has worked fairly well, but no thoughtful person can fail to be concerned by the problems which confront the department.

The sheer burden of the department's staying in touch with every interested element of the Congress, and still doing the rest of its job, is nearly reaching the point of physical impossibility. Almost every day the Congress is in session State Department officials will be formally testifying before one committee or another, and the careful preparation for these sessions is generally very time-consuming. In addition, for every formal session, there are each day countless informal conferences, briefings, and other contacts. Beyond that, congressional overseas travel is arranged; congressional constituents with relevant problems are received; State Department speakers are provided for functions in congressional districts; thousands of letters are prepared in response to congressional inquiries and the inquiries of congressional constituents each month; and it has been estimated that the Secretary and other senior officials spend anywhere from one sixth to one third or more of their time attending to congressional matters.

Related to the sheer physical burden of the consultative process is the problem of mechanics. At a time when the need is often greatest for rapid and effective action, the mechanics of consultation remain cumbersome and slow-moving.

Finally, there is the need for secrecy, as well as dispatch, in the conduct of effective diplomacy. This again presents a dilemma for the executive-congressional relationship in foreign-affairs matters. The requirement of secrecy is often in conflict with the need to consult frankly and fully with the large membership of both bodies of the Congress. A sensible executive will want the Congress involved in the take-offs, not just the crash landings, of foreign policy, but, given the numbers of the membership involved, this is never an easy thing to achieve.

Because of the numbers problem, success in the end will depend on more than executive willingness to consult and the development of ever-improving executive arrangements for this purpose. Critical, too, is a willingness on the part of Congress to face up to the need for improved internal organization and administrative arrangement in the area of its foreign-affairs responsibilities.

Organizationally backward as is the executive in these matters, the process of reorganization and modernization within its foreign-affairs community has been going on since World War II. During the same period, and despite the enormous new complexities and dimensions of the American foreign-affairs effort—and the congressional involvement in that effort—Congress has continued to operate within an administrative-organization structure, essentially unchanged, and designed for an earlier and simpler time. It has no coordinating National Security Council structure, or anything like it. It has no "question hour" that many parliaments use. Above all it presents no truly effective focal point with which the executive can deal in a definitive way. Out of the welter of its conflicting voices, it often cannot ascertain what its views really are, let alone bring these views to bear on the executive.

Modernization in the congressional structure is always more

difficult to achieve than it is in the executive. Both efforts inevitably face the opposition of vested interests, but the former depends on a difficult-to-achieve consensus, while the latter can ignore the need for consensus and rest largely instead on the determination and authority of one man, the President. Difficult as it is for the Congress systematically to overhaul its procedures, its failure to do so will surely compound the disadvantages and frustrations it already faces in seeking to exercise its influence in this critical area.

Congressional reform and modernization is not of course the responsibility of the diplomat. That must come from within the Congress itself, not from without. But the American diplomat and his fellow countrymen have an important stake in this enterprise, for an excessively frustrated Congress can be nothing but trouble to any foreign-affairs effort.

§

A last point to be made has to do with bipartisanship—or nonpartisanship, as Cordell Hull, one of its principal modern architects, used to prefer. It is a flawed but extremely valuable concept.

"Politics stops at the water's edge" is not a new idea; its present incarnation, however, dates its beginnings to World War II. It entails the development and maintenance of broad agreement between the two major American political parties on the general objectives and, in certain key areas, the specific tactics of American foreign policy.

It is a flawed concept because a fundamental precept of the American political system is that the two parties compete, rather than cooperate, with one another. As John Foster Dulles, an important wartime collaborator of Cordell Hull in the launching of this effort, has noted, the normal role of the two parties is to be watchdogs of one another, not teammates.

Bipartisanship requires sacrifices by both political parties. It means the majority party must defer to the minority party out of proportion to what the minority's political strength at the time would require. Inherent in the concept is the taking of time for minority persuasion and the making of adjustments to meet minority wishes, rather than simply outvoting them. It strengthens the hand of the minority beyond the point its strength in the body politic can justify. On the other hand, the sacrifice that the minority makes is considerable too. If the joint policy is successful it inevitably redounds at the next election time more to the credit of the incumbent party than to its opposition.

It is important to understand that bipartisanship does not mean an absence of controversy. The issues of foreign policy are much too important for that. What it means is a willingness on the part of both parties to exempt these issues from use for partisan purpose, to exclude them from partisan controversy and maneuver. Debate over them can, and often will, be intense indeed, but it should not be tied to party lines. In effect, what it means in the end is the formation of a coalition, made up of a majority of both parties, in support of certain key policy directions and undertakings.

Both because it is contrary to the basic tenets of the American political system and because it is so difficult to achieve (if it is successful it cuts across normal legislative-executive tension as well as rivalry between the two parties), it should be used only in the more important areas of the national foreign-policy effort.

Within these key areas, however, it can serve a valuable purpose indeed, well worth both the sacrifice of governmental theory and the often patience-trying difficulties involved. For, as has been noted earlier, predictability and stability of direction, especially on the part of the great powers, are key ingredients in the effort to produce a more stable world, and nothing can be more destabilizing than for the whole course of American foreign policy to hang in the balance every time there is an American presidential election. American diplomats should therefore always seek to persuade the leaders of the administration they currently serve of the importance of seeking bipartisan understanding and support for the fundamentals of the course it pursues—knowing full well that in the inevitable rhythm of American political life, the minority party will become the majority one day.

§

There is more, of course, that could usefully be discussed, but more than two hundred and fifty years ago, de Callières set standards of brevity for efforts of this kind which I am determined to emulate, if not to match. In any event, the things I most wished to say have now been said.

It remains only to reaffirm the conviction, implicit in all that has gone before, that in a selfish, predatory, dangerous, and explosive world the age-old effort to elevate the human condition and to liberate the human spirit can one day prevail—and that the necessary precondition to this, the establishment of a just and enduring peace, will one day be achieved.

But thousands of years of tragedy and suffering have shown that this essential precondition, this most persistently elusive of all human objectives, will not be achieved simply because decent people the world over wish it to be achieved. If human experience has taught us anything, it has taught us that. It requires instead a sustained, collective, resourceful, and, above all, hardheaded effort to deal with the world as it truly is; with a world whose realities are kept always in view, unmasked by the deadly distortions of illusion and wishful thinking.

In this great effort, diplomats from many lands will play their part. To do this well, to master with equal skill both the traditional and the ever changing requirements of their profession—and to do this while retaining a lifetime commitment to its true objectives—is what in essence the Angels' Game is all about.

Played with infinite skill and commitment, it can bring for its practitioners the incomparable satisfaction of knowing that one day, and in no small measure because of them,

> The latter glory of this place
> shall be greater than the former. . . .
> And in this place there shall
> be peace.

CHAPTER NOTES

CHAPTER ONE

§ For most countries, the term foreign ministry or foreign office is used to designate the government department which manages their foreign relations. In the United States, this department is called the State Department because in its earlier days, in addition to foreign-relations responsibilities, it carried out many of the domestic functions still performed at the state-government level by the secretaries of state of the various state governments. In this and succeeding chapters, the terms foreign ministry, foreign office, and State Department are used interchangeably.

§ The opening comment and quote concerning the alleged role of angels comes from Sir Harold Nicolson's *Diplomacy,* and it is appropriate that he should be the first author cited in any modern book on diplomacy. Much has changed in our profession since *Diplomacy* was prepared in the late 1930's; but much has not, and his book, which was to become such an important guide to so many diplomats in the ensuing years, remains of much value to this day. So, too, is his later, briefer *The Evolution of Diplomatic Method,* published by the Macmillan Company in 1954.

Unless otherwise noted, however, all references to Nicolson's writings contained in these chapter notes will be to his *Diplomacy* (Oxford University Press, 3d ed., 1970). The angels quote is from page 6.

§ The famous Sir Henry Wooten quote concerning "lying abroad" appears in almost any work on diplomacy. It was written in an album at Augsburg and word of it got back from there to Sir Henry's employer,

James I. I first came across the subsequent and less famous Wooten quote in Lord Strang's *Home and Abroad* (*Home and Abroad,* by Lord Strang, sometime Permanent Under Secretary of State for Foreign Affairs; André Deutsch Limited, 1956, page 17).

§ It is also most appropriate that François de Callières should, along with Nicholson, make such an early appearance. De Callières wrote more than two hundred years before Nicholson, but the latter in *Evolution* (page 62) says that de Callières's *On the Manner of Negotiating with Princes,* first published in 1716, "remains to this day the best manual of diplomatic method ever written." As one reads and rereads this classic of diplomatic literature—so notable not only for its continued timeliness and wisdom but also for its succinctness and brevity—one cannot fail to share Nicolson's admiration. If, out of all the literature of diplomacy, I could choose but two books to recommend to a newcomer to the profession, the two would be Nicolson's *Diplomacy* and de Callières's *On the Manner of Negotiating with Princes.* I have used A. F. Whyte's translation of the latter (University of Notre Dame Press, 1963), and all references to de Callières in these notes will be to that edition. De Callières's "rich opportunities" quote comes from page 146.

§ A sample of the range of definitions of "diplomacy":

> "Art and practice of conducting relations between nations, as in arranging treaties ... the business or art of conducting international intercourse..."
>
> —Webster's New International Dictionary
> (2d ed., 1957, G. & C. Merriam Company)

> The "ordered conduct of relations between one group of human beings and another group alien to themselves."
>
> —Nicolson

> "Diplomacy is the management of international relations by negotiation; the method by which these relations are adjusted and managed by ambassadors and envoys; the business or art of the diplomatist."
>
> —Oxford English Dictionary

> Diplomacy is "the application of intelligence and tact to the

conduct of official relations between the governments and independent states."

—Sir Ernest Satow, *Satow's Guide to*
Diplomatic Practice (4th ed., edited by
Sir Nevile Bland, Longmans, Green & Co., 1957), page 1

"Diplomacy is the art of resolving international difficulties
peacefully. It is also the technique or skill which reigns over the
development, in a harmonious manner, of international
relations."

Wood and Serres, *Diplomatic*
Ceremonial and Protocol (Columbia
University Press, New York, 1970), page 3

The object of the diplomat is "to bring about a harmonized union
between his master and the sovereign to whom he is sent. . . . He
must labour to remove misunderstandings, to prevent subjects of
dispute from arising, and generally to maintain in that foreign
country the honor and interests of his prince. This includes the
protection and patronage of his subjects, assistance to their business
enterprises, and the promotion of good relations between them
and the subjects of the foreign prince to whose court he is
accredited."

—De Callières, pages 111, 112

§ For a brief but authoritative description of diplomacy's historic
evolution, there is no better place to turn than Nicolson's *Diplomacy*.

§ The blunt reply of the Spartans to the ambassadors from Samos is
quoted by de Callières, page 64.

§ William Learned Marcy, like Sir Henry Wooten before him, is
remembered now primarily for one cynical pronouncement, despite the
fact that he, again like Wooten, said and did a number of useful things in
the course of a long and notable public career.

Marcy spoke from the Senate floor on a January day in 1832. He rose
in defense of the Jackson administration, and what he actually said was
"They see nothing wrong in the rule that to the victor belong the spoils of
the enemy."

Unlike Sir Henry, Marcy was not making a "mere merriment." He did not invent the spoils system, but he believed in it, and in that long-ago speech, he gave it its name. (See *Register of Debates*, 22d Congress, 1st Session, 1325.)

CHAPTER TWO

§ If one were given an opportunity to recommend three earlier writers to beginning diplomats, rather than just two, the choice, after de Callières and Nicolson, would indeed be a difficult one. Perhaps it should be Machiavelli. No modern diplomat should emulate him; but all should know what he said, and be forewarned. The Machiavellian mentality has by no means disappeared from the stage on which they must perform.

But Machiavelli aside, there is no clear third choice. My own, among many notable claimants, would be Charles W. Thayer, who like Nicolson left diplomacy in mid-career to become a full-time author. His *Diplomat* (Harper and Brothers, New York, 1959), from which all Thayer quotes in these chapters are taken, is written in a breezy, anecdotal, fast-paced style which tends to camouflage what a thoughtful and thorough book it really is.

§ De Callières wrote before some of the present dimensions of diplomacy were even dreamed of. Nicolson, and especially Thayer, wrote much closer to the event, but even in Thayer's time its dimensions, shape and impact were but dimly perceived. And to the extent they were perceived, they were not welcomed. It is presumptuous to seek to update such distinguished authorities, but because of the changes which have engulfed the profession, that is what is needed, and that is what this present effort attempts to do.

In any event, the reason Thayer's *Diplomat* comes up at this point is that he places the perceptive quote of the distinguished French diplomat Jules Cambon ("Unlike the military, the diplomat is not the spoiled child of history") on a separate page just following the introduction (written by Nicolson) and just before his first chapter begins.

In that introduction by Nicolson (page ix) one finds a particularly apt description of the American tendency to picture all diplomats as either snobbish lightweights or dangerous connivers. "There are those," he notes, "who regard the Foreign Service as a kind of bird sanctuary for elegant young men, with the milk of Groton still wet upon their lips, arrayed in striped pants and spending most of their time handing sugar cookies to ladies of high society in Europe and Latin America. Conversely, there are those who regard diplomatists as an international gang of intriguers. . . ."

§ In the Cyprus crisis which erupted on July 15, 1974, the United States lost still another of its hitherto unknown but highly professional diplomats, and many of us in the American embassy at Ankara lost not only a close neighbor but also a long-time colleague and friend. In the face of confusion and peril, Ambassador Rodger Davies manned his post in Cyprus with notable calmness, resourcefulness, and competence, until his life was cut short as a mob surrounded his embassy and a sniper attacked from a nearby building. All young diplomats should study his actions and his reporting from July 15 until his lifetime of service to the American people ended on August 19. Like the performance of Noel and Moore, the record of his final days constitutes a model of how a true professional acts under pressure.

CHAPTER THREE

§ There has been surprisingly little specific agreement among earlier writers on diplomacy as to the classic qualities and skills of the diplomat —except perhaps for two or three of the most obvious ones. Each authority has prepared a list, and each one is different in both content and emphasis. My own is drawn in part from some of these earlier listings and in part from what I have learned from my own experiences and from that of my contemporaries.

Focus on the new, added requirements of the profession has been sufficiently recent that in most earlier instances they have been left off the lists altogether.

§ The quote in this chapter from Thayer can be found on page 240 of *Diplomat.* Jules Cambon's words are quoted on the same page. They are also quoted by Nicolson on page 58 of *Diplomacy.*

§ Thomas A. Bailey in his *Art and Practice of Diplomacy* (Appleton-Century-Crofts, 1968) addresses the subject of integrity in diplomacy, and (page 75) employs a different quote from Cavour: "European diplomacy," Bailey writes, "was traditionally more or less synonymous with duplicity: To lie and deny were among the envoy's first duties. He was not only a licensed spy, but a licensed liar. . . . The French King Louis XI instructed his envoys 'If they lie to you, lie still more to them.' 'Accredited mendacity' became so much the norm that Count Cavour, the 19th Century Italian statesman, reported, 'I have discovered the art of deceiving diplomats. I speak the truth and they never believe me.'" Machiavelli's quote is also cited by Bailey, among others, and comes from chapter 18 of *The Prince.*

§ De Callières's quotes used in this chapter come from pages 13 and 130 of *On the Manner of Negotiating with Princes.*

§ The famous letter of Sir James Harris (Lord Malmesbury) is dated April 11, 1813. It was written to Lord Camden, who had asked for advice to pass on to his nephew, who was entering the diplomatic service. The letter is from Malmesbury's *Diaries and Correspondence,* IV, page 420, and is quoted in full in Sir Ernest Satow's *Guide to Diplomatic Practice* (4th ed.), page 97. The reference to his being, in Talleyrand's judgment, the greatest foreign envoy of his time comes from Nicolson (page 31), who quotes Talleyrand as saying, "I hold him to be the ablest Minister of his time—it was impossible to surpass him, all one could do was to follow him as closely as possible." Nicolson does not give him such high marks, and he is particularly unimpressed with the results of Malmesbury's attempted boudoir diplomacy, and other efforts to suborn, at the court of Catherine the Great.

§ Nicolson's comment on moral inaccuracies is found on page 16 of *Diplomacy.*

§ Monsieur de Faber's reproach to Mazarin is quoted, with approval, by de Callières, page 34.

§ Talleyrand's "*Et surtout pas trop de zèle*" turns up almost always in any discussion of diplomatic method. Thayer (page 244) calls it the "best known advice to diplomats."

Similarly, the Dawes quote is well known. It can be found in *That Man Dawes* by Paul R. Leach, page 326. Henry P. Fletcher, according to Bailey (footnote on page 38), was the former American diplomat to whom the riposte is credited.

§ The John Kenneth Galbraith quote comes from his *Economics, Peace & Laughter,* Houghton Mifflin, 1971, page 93.

§ On the subject of self-control, de Callières, pages 34–35 and 108, has, as always, something useful to say. "A man who is naturally violent and easily carried away, is ill fitted to the conduct of negotiations; it is almost impossible for him to be master of himself at those critical moments, and unforeseeen occasions when the command of one's temper is of importance, especially at the acute moments of diplomatic controversy. . . ." And again, ". . . he must preserve a calm and resolute mind when events conspire against him. . . ."

CHAPTER FOUR

§ The de Callières quotes used in this chapter come from *On the Manner of Negotiating with Princes*, page 134.

§ The Thomas Jefferson quote is from a letter he wrote to William Carmichael, American chargé in Spain, on November 6, 1791. It is used at the start of a Senate study entitled *Administration of National Security: The American Ambassador*, a study prepared by the (Jackson) Subcommittee on Government Operations, U.S. Senate, 88th Congress, 2d Session.

§ The quote from the early U.S. consular regulations comes from *General Instructions to the Consuls and Commercial Agents of the United States: 1838*, page 23.

§ The Satow quote is from *Satow's Guide to Diplomatic Practice*, page 101.

CHAPTER FIVE

§ The Nicolson quote at the start of this chapter is from *Diplomacy*, page 60. His opposition to summit diplomacy is outlined on page 52.

§ The Napoleon quote comes from *The Mind of Napoleon*, edited by J. C. Herold (1955), page 170.

§ The de Callières quote comes from *On the Manner . . .*, page 110.

§ The Malmesbury quote is from Sato, page 97.

CHAPTER SIX

§ The quote concerning the new importance of understanding a nation, as compared with the earlier importance of persuading a prince or his minister, comes from J. J. Jusserand's *The School for Ambassadors* (1925), page 59. Jusserand was the French ambassador in Washington for over twenty years.

§ The Churchill quote, the first part of which is so much better known than its last sentence, comes from a speech broadcast on October 1, 1939.

CHAPTER EIGHT

§ The William Graham Sumner quote comes from *Essays of William Graham Sumner,* Yale University Press (1934), I, pages 169ff.

§ The "intellectual exhaustion" and "the risks always outweigh the opportunities" quotes come from Arthur M. Schlesinger, Jr.'s, *A Thousand Days* (Houghton Mifflin, 1965), pages 414ff. The immediately following Nicolson quote is from *Diplomacy,* page 65.

§ Edward Barton was the Elizabethan trader-diplomat. His dual role is noted in Noel Barber's *Lords of the Golden Horn* (Macmillan, 1973), page 71. David Offley played an important role in early U.S.-Turkey relations, and appears in any book on this subject.

CHAPTERS NINE THROUGH TWELVE

§ "First-rate people having to operate in a third-rate system" is a phrase I first heard from my friend Charles Bray, who employed it often in the days when he was the "young Turk" president of the American Foreign Service Association.

§ Even as intelligent an observer as Thayer endorses the comment by substantive diplomatic officers about administrative officers being valets who "instead of pressing our pants . . . are inclined to wear them." "Tactless as this remark may have been," he writes, "it was not unjustified." *Diplomat,* page 274.

§ The statement that it was undignified for a king to be represented by a woman is found in A. de Wicquefort's *L'Ambassadeur et ses fonctions* (London, 1840), part 2, page 96.

§ Those who have a special interest in the management side of modern diplomacy—discussed in these four chapters—may find it useful to refer to *Diplomacy for the 70's: A Program of Management Reform for the Department of State,* published by the U.S. Government Printing Office (as Department of State Publication 8551), 1970. This reports on the work of thirteen major task forces, which functioned at the time I was serving as the chief administrative officer of the department. With a strong mandate from then Secretary William Rogers and then Under Secretary Elliot Richardson, these task forces were charged with first looking into all the department's ills, and then prescribing detailed remedies.

The unique aspect of this effort (in contrast to earlier reform efforts) was that the task forces were made up almost entirely of substantive, active-duty State Department and Foreign Service personnel, with the remaining places being filled by active-duty professionals from those other departments and agencies most closely associated with the State Department in the U.S. government's foreign-affairs community. They were not "experts" in the sense that outsiders brought in to staff such efforts usually are. They were charged, however, with consulting outside experts, and with reviewing the many valuable—but largely unimplemented—management recommendations that had been prepared through the years by these experts.

The theory behind this approach was twofold. First was the belief that after carefully studying the problems, which many of these active-duty professionals had never really done, their conclusions and recommendations were likely to be very close to those that the experts had been urging for some time—and that to the extent that they differed their views were likely to be sounder and more thorough, coming as they did from persons who now had both the outsider's expertise and the insider's knowledge of the system.

On the whole, this first assumption proved correct. The approximately 250 professionals who served on the task forces were among the most able in the service, and their product, while uneven, was remarkably perceptive and constructive. It also benefited from the insider's license to be critical. It said things which needed to be said and which, coming from insiders, were far less resented than they would have otherwise been.

The second aspect of the theory behind this insider approach is related to this last point. It was thought that criticism and recommendations coming from an inside effort would be much less resisted, and would be much easier to implement, than identical criticism and recommendations from outsiders. That, too, proved to be the case—but by no means to the point where anyone subsequently involved in the implementing process was not daily reminded that, no matter what the circumstances, devising solutions is easier than implementing them.

The report of the task forces is some six hundred pages in length, but it is usefully summarized in its first thirty pages. The keynote speech which launched this effort is printed in the appendix. In abbreviated form, I first touched there on many of the management themes discussed in chapters 9 through 11.

§ For a perceptive analysis of the management challenges faced by the State Department, and of other earlier efforts to deal with them, see also John Harr's excellent *The Professional Diplomat* (Princeton University Press, 1969).

§ There is an additional impelling and obvious reason, not mentioned in chapter 10, for the prompt development of more effective managerial systems than are now possessed by state departments and foreign offices, to arrive at agreed-upon priorities. New requirements, new objectives, are constantly being assigned to all government departments, and the traditional procedure is to make these additive to the collection of demands and objectives which these departments have already accumulated. This in turn traditionally means either that endlessly increasing numbers of personnel must be added to the government payroll, or that the same number of persons are left to do more and more things less and less well. Neither solution, of course, is acceptable. Instead, the answer lies in systematically identifying precise priorities and, as new ones of a higher order are added, in being prepared to lop off some of the older ones of lesser priority.

The question to be asked of each activity, then, is not whether it is useful and important. Bureaucrats, including diplomats, can almost always (and often correctly) explain why something they have been doing is both. The question is not whether this is so, but rather how important and how useful is any particular activity in comparison with rival activities now levying other claims on the finite, rather than infinite, time and energies of their parent organization.

§ On the subject of seventh-floor staff, it is a source of concern that in many foreign offices the policy-planning group and the senior budget staff so often seem to operate so independently of each other. (In the U.S. State Department, for example, these two staffs were for many years both physically and figuratively at the opposite ends of the seventh floor.) Yet the work of each is essential to the other. Budget planning, to be relevant, must be tied to policy. Policy planning, to be effective, must impact directly on budget allocations. And policy planners will be taken far more seriously by other components of a foreign ministry whenever it becomes clear that their views have a controlling weight with the budget office.

§ The genesis of the Secretary of the Year award dated back to the days when, as a young officer, I first observed the work of so many very able secretaries, and when I first became conscious of how critically they affect the quality of an institution's performance. By the time I was in a position to have the award created, the person who, through her distinguished performance as secretary to two secretaries of state, had become its principal inspiration (and to whom this book is dedicated) was no longer eligible to receive it. I continue to think of it, however, as her award.

§ As a footnote to the discussion of employee-management relations, it is perhaps worth adding the injunction that diplomats should never permit any employee-management relations system from being turned into an exercise exclusively in "What's in it for me?" If they do, then something very valuable will have disappeared from the spirit of their service. Unfortunately, this point can be turned into unfair and improper argument against employee-diplomats in almost any dispute with management. The fact that on occasion it can be misused by one side, however, does not mean that on no occasion should it be considered by the other.

CHAPTER THIRTEEN

§ The quotes from de Callières are from pages 59, 57, 81, 66, and 144.

§ The Sir Ernest Satow quote comes from his *Satow's Guide to Diplomatic Practice*, page 99.

§ In this chapter the argument is strongly advanced that the number of "noncareer" ambassadorial appointments should be sharply curtailed, and the number of "career" appointments significantly increased. With respect to the latter, however, the career base should be broadened, and more outstanding career officers from other parts of the government's foreign-affairs community should be chosen for chiefs of mission than is now the case. While the bulk of the career ambassadorial appointments should, of course, continue to come from the diplomatic service, able and seasoned careerists from other closely associated departments and agencies—especially those with extensive and successful embassy "country team" experience—should be put more into the competition for these jobs than is presently the case. In this way the talent base from which to select these critically important appointees can be expanded to include all—not just the most obvious portion—of the experienced career talent available.

§ The Thayer account of the highly undiplomatic reply is found in *Diplomat*, page 56.

§ British Foreign Minister Sir Edward Grey's "George the Third" remark comes from *The Life and Letters of Walter H. Page* by Burton J. Hendrick (New York, 1922), I, page 391.

§ *"La véritable finesse est la vérité dite quelquefois avec force, toujours avec grâce"*—True finesse is the truth spoken sometimes with force, always with grace. Attributed to the Duc de Choiseul by Graham H. Stewart, *American Diplomatic and Consular Practice* (2d ed., Appleton-Century-Crofts, 1952), page 171.

§ The John Bassett Moore quote is from "John Bassett Moore," *Digest of International Law* (1906), IV, page 707.

§ The long-ago instructions about receiving gifts come from *U.S. Consular Instructions: 1838,* page 25, article 46.

§ William Learned Marcy reappears in this chapter. The spoils of office clearly in his view did not include the wearing of fancy diplomatic uniforms. Nineteen years after his famous declaration on the Senate floor, it was he, as secretary of state, who issued the June 1, 1853, instruction regarding the "simple dress of an American citizen."

§ The Joseph Choate quote regarding "this republican simplicity dodge" is cited by Stuart (page 216) and attributed to *Life of Whitelaw Reid* by Royal Cortissoz (New York, 1921), II, page 351. Choate, among others, is alleged to be the plainly dressed American diplomat who, at the conclusion of a diplomatic function, was mistaken for a servant and imperiously asked by another, more resplendently costumed, diplomat that he call him a cab. Obligingly the American complied. "You are a cab," he said. Later, he is alleged to have told friends it would have been politer to have said, "You are a hansom cab."

§ The Duke of Wellington's alleged message to headquarters was told me by a British military friend but I have no other citation for it.

CHAPTERS FOURTEEN AND FIFTEEN

§ The Congressional appropriations subcommittee testimony comes from hearings before chairman Otto Passman in 1964, when, as an assistant administrator in the U.S. Agency for International Development, I was defending the agency's appropriation request for the Near East and South Asia.

§ The Chip Bohlen quote which opens Chapter 15 is from *Witness to History 1929–1969* by Charles E. Bohlen (W. W. Norton, 1973), page 7.

§ The Corwin quote can be found in *The President: Office and Powers* (3d ed., revised, New York University, 1948), page 208.

§ The Acheson quote comes from *A Citizen Looks at Congress* by Dean Acheson (Harper and Bros., copyright by Dean Acheson 1956, 1957).

§ The concluding words of the book come from the biblical prophet Haggai (2:9). Spoken originally in connection with the rebuilding of the temple in Jerusalem, they are found today at Coventry, England, on the site where the new cathedral stands, next to the shell of its predecessor, destroyed in the bombing raids of World War II. Haggai was a minor prophet who spoke four times in 520 B.C. and then disappeared from history's view. Regarded as colorless in his literary style, he nonetheless in these few words speaks movingly for our times as well as his own.

GLOSSARY OF DIPLOMATIC TERMS *

ACCESSION: The procedure by which a nation becomes a party to an agreement already in force between other nations.

ACCORDS: International agreements originally thought to be for lesser subjects than covered by treaties, but now really treaties by a different name.

AD REFERENDUM: An agreement reached ad referendum means an agreement reached by negotiators at the table, subject to the subsequent concurrence of their governments.

AGRÉMENT: Diplomatic courtesy requires that before a state appoints a new chief of diplomatic mission to represent it in another state, it must be first ascertained whether the proposed appointee is acceptable to the receiving state. The acquiescence of the receiving state is signified by its granting its agrément to the appointment. It is unusual for an agrément to be refused, but it occasionally happens.

ALTERNAT: When an agreement is signed between two states, or among several states, each signatory keeps an official copy for itself. Alternat refers to the principle which provides that a state's own name will be listed ahead of the other signatory, or signatories, in

---

* Many terms and phrases familiar to earlier generations of diplomats have now dropped from general use. This present listing includes older terms which have, to varying degrees, endured, as well as modern phrases (e.g., country team) unknown to diplomats of other times. The prevalence of Latin and French terms is a reflection of the fact that for many years Latin and French were, *seriatim*, the languages of diplomacy. Authoritative sources consulted have been Sir Ernest Satow's *Guide to Diplomatic Practice* (Longmans, 4th ed.); Sir Harold Nicolson's *Diplomacy* (Oxford University Press, 3d ed.); *Webster's New International Dictionary* (G. & C. Merriam Company); and the *U.S. State Department's Correspondence Handbook*.

its own official copy. It is a practice devised centuries ago to handle sensitivities over precedence.

AIDE MÉMOIRE: A written summary of the key points made by a diplomát in an official conversation. Literally, a document left with the other party to the conversation, either at the time of the conversation or subsequently, as an aid to memory.

AMBASSADOR EXTRAORDINARY AND PLENIPOTENTIARY: The chief of diplomatic mission; the ranking official diplomatic representative of his country to the country to which he is accredited, and the personal representative of his own head of state to the head of state of the host country.

The term "extraordinary" has no real meaning. Years ago it was given only to nonresident ambassadors on temporary missions and was used to distinguish them from regular resident ambassadors. The latter resented others having this appellation, as it seemed to imply a lesser position for themselves. Eventually, therefore, it was accorded to them as well. "Plenipotentiary" also comes down through the years. Today it simply means possessed of full power to do an ambassador's normal job.

AMBASSADOR-DESIGNATE: An official who has been named to be an ambassador, but who has not yet taken his oath of office.

AMBASSADRESS: A term often used to denote the wife of an ambassador, and misused to denote a woman chief of mission. The latter is an ambassador, not an ambassadress.

ASYLUM: Used in diplomacy to mean the giving of refuge in two senses: first, within the extraterritorial grounds of an embassy (not generally done in American embassies); and second, when one state allows someone to live within its borders, out of reach of the authority of a second state from which the person seeks protection.

ATTACHÉ: Civilian attachés are either junior officers in an embassy or, if more senior, officers who have a professional specialization such as "labor attaché," "commercial attaché," "cultural attaché," etc. On the military side, an embassy will generally have either an army attaché, naval attaché, or air attaché—and often all three. In American embassies, the senior of the three is called the defense attaché and is in charge of all military attaché activities. These consist largely of liaison work with local military authorities and of keeping informed on host country order of battle.

BAG, THE: See "Pouch." Bag is the British term. "Bag day" is the day the pouch is sealed and sent to the home office. Hence, bag day is the day when all nontelegraphic reporting must be finalized and dispatched.

BELLIGERENCY: A state of belligerency is a state of armed conflict. Belligerents are direct participants in that conflict.

BILATERAL: Bilateral discussions or negotiations are between a state and one other. A bilateral treaty is between a state and one other. "Multilateral" is used when more than two states are involved.

BOUT DE PAPIER: A very informal means of conveying written information; more informal than an aide mémoire or a memorandum.

BREAKING RELATIONS: The formal act of severing diplomatic relations with another state to underscore disapproval of its actions or policies. It is generally an unwise step, because when relations between states are most strained is when the maintaining of diplomatic relations is most important. It makes little sense to keep diplomats on the scene when things are going relatively well and then take them away when they are most needed. An intermediate step which indicates serious displeasure but stops short of an actual diplomatic break is for a government to recall its ambassador indefinitely. This is preferable to a break in relations as his embassy will continue to function; but again this comes under the heading of cutting off one's nose to spite one's face. If a dramatic gesture of this kind is needed, it is far better promptly and publicly to recall an ambassador for consultations, and then just as promptly return him to his post.

CALLS AND CALLING CARDS: "Calling" has largely disappeared from private life, but it is a practice which is still useful in a diplomatic community where the early establishment of extensive contacts is a must. Soon after a diplomat's arrival at a new post, therefore, he will embark on a program of calls on those with whom he will be dealing—and whom he must lose no time in getting to know.

In modern, less formal times, calling cards do not have nearly the same role in diplomatic life they once did. But with the traditional initials, p.p. (*pour présenter*); p.f. (*pour féliciter*); p.c. (*pour condoléance*); p.r. (*pour remercier*); or p.p.c. (*pour prendre congé*) inscribed at their bottom left-hand corner, they remain a still useful and accepted way to convey simple messages of presentation, congratulation, condolence, thanks, and farewell.

CASUS BELLI: An action by one state regarded as so contrary to the interests of another state as to be considered by that second state a a cause for war.

CHANCELLERIES: As in "chancelleries of Europe," i.e. foreign offices.

CHANCERY: The office where the chief of mission and his staff work. This office is often called the embassy but this is a misnomer. Technically, the embassy is where the ambassador lives, not where he works, although in earlier times when diplomatic missions were smaller, this was usually the same building. Today, for clarity's sake, many diplomats now distinguish between the two by using the terms "embassy residence" and "embassy office."

CHANCERY, HEAD OF: An important position in British embassies not found in American diplomatic establishments. An officer, usually head of the political section, charged with coordinating the substantive and administrative performance of the embassy. In an American embassy, the ambassador looks to the deputy chief of mission to do this.

CHARGÉ D'AFFAIRES, A.I.: Formerly, a chargé d'affaires was the title of a chief of mission, inferior in rank to an ambassador or a minister. Today with the a.i. (*ad interim*) added, it designates the senior officer taking charge for the interval when a chief of mission is absent from his post.

CHIEF OF MISSION: The ranking officer in an embassy, permanent mission, legation, consulate general or consulate (i.e., an ambassador always, and a minister, consul general, or consul when no more senior officer is assigned to the post). A "chief of mission" can also be the head of a special and temporary diplomatic mission, but the term is usually reserved for the earlier listed examples.

CLEARANCES: A message or other document conveying a policy or an instruction is "cleared" in a foreign office, or large embassy, when all officials who have responsibility for any of its specific aspects have signified their approval by initialing it. Some officers gain a reputation for insisting on changing, even if only in minor ways, everything that is placed before them—and it is occasionally alleged they would do so even if it were the Ten Commandments being presented to them. Conversely, others are occasionally so casual that their clearance seems to mean only that the document in question does not appear to take away any of their jurisdiction. A clearance procedure in some form is essential for adequate coordination, but when overdone (as it often is), it can be a stifling, time-consuming process, and a bane of diplomatic life.

COMMUNIQUÉ: A brief public summary statement issued following important bilateral or multilateral meetings. These tend to be bland and full of stock phrases such as "full and frank discussions," and the like. Occasionally, getting agreement on the communiqué turns out to be the most difficult part of the meeting.

CONCILIATION: An effort to achieve agreement and, hopefully, increased good will between two opposed parties.

CONCORDAT: A treaty to which the Pope is a party.

CONFERENCE OR CONGRESS: International meetings. In the diplomatic sense, a congress has the same meaning as a conference.

CONSULAR AGENT: An official doing consular work for a nation in a locality where it does not maintain a regular consulate. This official is usually a national of his host state, and his work is usually part-time.

CONSULATE: An office established by one state in an important city of another state for the purpose of supporting and protecting its citizens traveling or residing there. In addition, these offices are charged with performing other important administrative duties such as issuing visas (where this is required) to host country nationals wishing to travel to the country the consulate represents.

All consulates, whether located in the capital city or in other communities, are administratively under the ambassador and the embassy. In addition to carrying out their consular duties, they often serve as branch offices for the embassy, supporting, for example, the latter's political and economic responsibilities. Consulates are expected to play a particularly significant role in connection with the promotion of their own country's exports and other commercial activities. Officers performing consular duties are known as consuls, or, if more junior, vice consuls. The chief of the consulate is known as *the* consul.

CONSULATE GENERAL: A bigger and more important consulate, presided over by a consul general.

CONSUL, HONORARY: A host-country national appointed by a foreign state to perform limited consular functions in a locality where the appointing state has no other consular representation.

CONVENTION: An agreement between two or more states, often more, concerning matters of common interest. While supposedly used for lesser matters than embraced in a treaty, it often deals with important subjects indeed—international postal and copyright laws, for example, or the law of the sea.

COUNSELOR OF EMBASSY: A senior diplomatic title ranking just behind an ambassador and a minister. In many embassies there is no minister, and the counselor is the number two man, i.e., the deputy chief of mission. (In a very small embassy, the second man may not have this rank.) In a large embassy, the second ranking officer may be a minister, or minister-counselor, in which case the heads of the more important sections have counselor rank. Thus, for example, the embassy's political counselor, economic counselor, and administrative counselor are well-known and much-respected positions in diplomatic life.

COUNTRY DESK: State departments and foreign offices generally have an office for each country with which they have active dealings. These offices are often called country desks, and if a large country is involved and there is a large embassy to support there, the desk is likely to be staffed by a large number of officers. A smaller country may require a one-officer desk only.

COUNTRY TEAM: An American diplomatic term meaning the ambassador's cabinet. It consists of his deputy chief of mission, heads of all important embassy sections, and the chiefs of all other elements (military, agricultural, aid, information, and cultural, etc.) working under him in the "embassy community."

CREDENTIALS: The name for letters given to an ambassador by his chief of state, and addressed to the chief of state of his host country. They are delivered to the latter by ambassadors in a formal credentials ceremony, which generally takes place shortly after his arrival at a new post. Until this ceremony has taken place he is not formally recognized by the host country, and he cannot officially act as ambassador. The letters are termed "letters of credence" because they request the receiving chief of state to give "full credence" to what the ambassador will say on behalf of his government.

D.C.M.: Embassy shorthand for the deputy chief of mission.

DECLARATION: This can have two quite distinct meanings in diplomacy. It can first, of course, mean a unilateral statement by one state, ranging from an expression of opinion or policy to a declaration of war. It can also mean a joint statement by two or more states having the same binding effect as a treaty. In this latter connection declarations can be put forward either in their own right or appended to a treaty as an added understanding or interpretation.

DELEGATION: Again used in two senses in diplomacy. "Delegation" can be the term used to refer to the specific powers delegated by his government to a diplomat acting in certain specific circumstances. It also refers to an official party sent to an international conference or on some other special diplomatic mission.

DÉMARCHE: An approach, a making of representations. Still a very common term used by diplomats to indicate the official raising of a matter with host country officials, often accompanied by a specific request for some type of action or decision in connection with it.

DÉTENTE: An easing of tension between states.

DIPLOMATIC CORPS: The body of foreign diplomats assembled at a nation's capital. In cities where consuls and consuls general are resident, they are collectively referred to as the consular corps. The dean of both corps is usually that official who has been at his post the longest. There are exceptions to this latter rule, however. For example, in some Catholic countries, the papal nuncio is always the dean. The dean represents the corps in its collective dealings with host country officials on matters of a ceremonial or administrative character affecting the corps as a whole.

DIPLOMATIC ILLNESS: The practice of feigning illness to avoid participation in a diplomatic event of one kind or another and at the same time to avoid giving formal offense. "Diplomatic deafness" is a somewhat related concept whereby older diplomats allegedly turn this infirmity to advantage by not hearing what they prefer not to hear.

DIPLOMATIC PRIVILEGES AND IMMUNITIES: Historically accorded in recognition that the diplomat represents (and is responsible to) a different sovereignty; also in order that the legitimate pursuit of his official duties will not be impeded in any unnecessary way.

They include inviolability of person and premises and exemption from taxation and the civil and criminal jurisdiction of local courts.

DIPLOMATIST: It has the same meaning as "diplomat." An outdated word rarely used now in spoken diplomacy but occasionally still appearing in the literature of diplomacy.

DISPATCH: A written, as opposed to a telegraphic, message from an embassy to its home office or vice versa.

ECONOMIC OFFICER: A career diplomat who specializes in economics rather than political, administrative, or other matters.

EMBASSY: The residence of an ambassador. In recent years, also inaccurately used to denote the building which contains the offices of the ambassador and other key members of his staff. The proper term for the latter, as noted above, is the "chancery." As also noted above, confusion is nowadays avoided through the practice of using the two terms "embassy residence" and "embassy office."

ENTENTE: Denotes a close understanding between certain nations. It suggests mutual and complementary efforts, and a sense of compatible objectives. It can be agreed on orally or in writing, but as a concept is generally less binding than a treaty relationship.

ENVOY: Nowadays used to refer to any senior diplomat. Earlier it had a specific hierarchical connotation, being used to designate diplomatic agents of less than the highest rank.

EXCELLENCY: An archaic but still much-used title for addressing an ambassador. Theoretically, an American ambassador is not supposed to be addressed this way, but he generally is—along with all his other ambassadorial colleagues. "Mr. Ambassador" is more accurate and less silly. That he is; he may or may not be "excellent."

EXCHANGE OF NOTES: A common way of recording an agreement. The contents of the notes are, of course, agreed upon in advance by the two nations participating in the exchange.

EXEQUATUR: A document issued to a consul by the host country government authorizing him to carry out his consular duties.

EX GRACIA: Something which is done as a gesture of good will and not on the basis of an accepted legal obligation.

EXTRADITION: The term for the process, governed by formally concluded agreements, by which fugitives from justice in one country are returned from the country where they have sought refuge. It does not apply to political offenses.

EXTRATERRITORIALITY: The exercise by one nation, as a result of formally concluded agreements, of certain sovereign functions within the territory of another state. A curtailment of the jurisdiction of the latter state in certain specified areas and/or in certain specified respects.

FINAL ACT (ACTE FINAL): A formal summary statement, drawn up at the conclusion of a conference.

FOGGY BOTTOM: The name given to a once marshlike area near Washington's Potomac River, and now somewhat irreverently bequeathed to the U.S. Department of State, one of that area's best-known modern occupants.

FOREIGN AFFAIRS COMMUNITY: An American government term used to denote the State Department and other government departments and agencies (Defense, Commerce, Agriculture, Treasury, U. S. Information Agency, the Central Intelligence Agency, the Agency for International Development, etc.) which have special interests and responsibilities in the foreign affairs field.

F.S.O.: Shorthand for a career American diplomat, i.e., an American Foreign Service officer.

FULL POWERS: A document which authorizes a diplomat to conduct and consummate special business on behalf of his government, such as the settlement of a dispute or the negotiation and signing of a treaty. Before signing a treaty, a diplomat is obligated to show his full-powers document to the other parties involved.

GOOD OFFICES: An effort by a third state, or by an individual or an international body, designed to stimulate the processes of settlement in a dispute between two other states.

GUARANTEE, TREATY OF: A treaty which requires the signatories to guarantee that situations agreed upon will be maintained. The honoring of such commitments can precipitate armed conflicts.

LEGATION: These are rare now, but they were once very common. A legation is a diplomatic mission similar for most practical purposes to an embassy, but lower in rank, and presided over by a minister rather than an ambassador. For most of the last century,

American diplomatic representation abroad was limited to legations, and for much of this century, the U.S. was represented in more countries by legations than it was by embassies.

LETTERS OF CREDENCE: See Credentials.

LETTERS OF RECALL: Also presented by a new ambassador, along with his letters of credence, to the chief of state of his host country during his credentials-presentation ceremony. It is the official document which formally recalls his predecessor.

MINISTER, MINISTER-COUNSELOR: Apart from its cabinet-officer connotation (i.e., "foreign minister"), a minister has traditionally been a chief of diplomatic mission who headed a legation rather than an embassy. As so few legations are left, the title is now borrowed more and more to designate the second-ranking officer of a large embassy. It has, therefore, come increasingly to mean the senior counselor under the ambassador. To avoid confusion with the old connotation, the United States and a number of other governments designate these senior deputy chiefs of mission by the hyphenated title "minister-counselor."

MODUS VIVENDI: A temporary agreement, in writing, of an interim character, pending the negotiation of more definitive arrangements.

NATIONAL: Generally used to mean a citizen, i.e., a national of country X is a citizen of that country.

NOTES, DIPLOMATIC: While today communications between states are often not as formally structured as they once were, diplomatic notes remain a key means by which they conduct written business with each other.

Notes take a number of different forms. There are highly formal and stylized first-person notes sent by an ambassador to a foreign minister, or vice versa. There are far less stylized notes, again in the first person, employed by each on less formal occasions and closely resembling ordinary letters.

There are a range of third-person notes, the most common of which is a *note verbale*. These are unsigned, but initialed, and have the same function as notes of a more formal variety. Because they are considered more informal, they are the most used. And despite their more informal character, they still commonly begin with the words: "The Ambassador of country X presents his compliments to his Excellency, the Minister of Foreign Affairs of country Y (or the Embassy of country X presents its compliments to the Ministry of Foreign Affairs) and has the honor to. . ."

Other types of notes are: 1) *circular notes,* bearing the same message from an ambassador to a number of chiefs of mission of the resident diplomatic corps; 2) *collective notes,* which are joint representations by two or more senders to one or more addressees, containing identical texts (these are rare in diplomacy as they tend to suggest a ganging up by the sending states which receiving states may find offensive); and 3) *identic notes,* representing a less offensive form of collective notes; less offensive because, while they have a similar substantive content, neither their language nor their timing is identical.

NOTE, DIPLOMATIC, REJECTION OF: The act of refusing to accept a note, or of insisting on its physical return to the originator, because of its offensive contents.

NUNCIO: A diplomatic chief of mission of ambassadorial rank, representing the Vatican. A Vatican representative of ministerial rank is an internuncio.

PASSPORT: A travel identity document, officially issued to a citizen by his government, which verifies his citizenship, asks other governments to accord prompt and unhindered passage and, where needed, aid and protection.

PERSONA NON GRATA: When a host governmemt so declares a diplomat accredited to it, that diplomat must leave. The host government does not have to give any reason for taking this drastic action. It can be done through quietly passing word to the sending state that a change would be appreciated. Or it can be done by abruptly expelling the diplomat in question. To be "P.N.G.'d" is a serious blot on a diplomat's record unless his own government believes the reasons the action was taken against him were baseless.

POLITICAL OFFICER: A career diplomat who specializes in political rather than economic, consular, administrative, or other matters.

POUCH: A sealed bag used to transport nontelegraphic communications, publications, and the like from foreign offices to embassies and vice versa. Pouches carrying classified material are accompanied by a diplomatic courier. They are shipped by air or by sea or rail, depending on their urgency, and are immune from search by foreign officials.

PROCÈS-VERBAL: Originally this term referred to summary minutes of the proceedings of an international conference, subsequently formalized by the signatures of the participants. It is now used primarily as a device to give official notice of treaty ratifications.

PRO MEMORIA: A memorandum covering points under discussion. Less formal than a note.

PROTECTING POWER: When diplomatic relations are severed between two states, each selects a third state to look after its interests in the other's capital. This entails not only its property interests (vacated embassy, chancery, staff residences and their equipment, etc.) but also on occasion its diplomatic interests as well. Activities of the latter type are, of course, much curtailed, but sometimes they remain sufficiently active that a state which no longer has formal diplomatic relations will send its own diplomatic officials to staff the "interests section" within this third-country embassy now looking after its affairs. The latter can be done, of course, only with the approval of the host government.

PROTOCOL: Refers to the ceremonial side of diplomacy, including matters of diplomatic courtesy and precedence.

PROTOCOL: Another name for an agreement. Originally a protocol was considered a somewhat less formal document than a treaty, but that is a distinction no longer valid. A protocol may be an agreement in its own right. It also may constitute added sections which clarify or alter an agreement, or it may be used to add new subjects of agreement to the original document.

RAPPORTEUR: The official of a committee or subcommittee whose job is to prepare a summary report of its discussions and conclusions.

RAPPROCHEMENT: The establishment of improved relations.

RATIFICATION: The act, subseqent to a treaty's having been negotiated, by which a government commits itself to adhere to that treaty. In the United States, it is inaccurate to speak of the Senate's ratifying a treaty. The executive does this, but only after the Senate has given its consent.

RECOGNITION: Commonly used in connection with the recognition by one state of 1) the existence of another state (for example when a new one is formed), or 2) the existence of a government which is in effective control of a state. The term "de facto recognition" means recognition that a state, or a government of a state, in fact exists—but it also means the withholding of full official recognition of this. When the latter is extended, it is termed "de jure recognition." It is a distinction based more on diplomatic convenience than on logic.

SEVENTH FLOOR: Shorthand for the most senior leadership of the U.S. State Department. It is where the offices of the Secretary of State and his most senior aides are located.

SHORT-TIMER: A diplomat whose assignment at a foreign post is nearing its close. A phrase borrowed from the military.

SIXTH FLOOR: Where many of the U.S. State Department's regional and other assistant secretaries have their offices. Shorthand for the assistant secretary level of the department's leadership.

T.D.Y.: Shorthand for a temporary duty assignment.

TOUR D'HORIZON: A diplomatic discussion covering most (or at least a number of) subjects of current and common concern.

TREATY: A formal mutually binding agreement between countries. The term comes from *traiter*, to negotiate.

ULTIMATUM: A last statement indicating a final position. On occasion a prelude to the initiation of military action.

UNFRIENDLY ACT: A term used when one government wishes to tell another that an action the latter has taken is regarded as so serious that it might lead to a military action against it. An action which risks war.

VISA: Written authority to enter a country for either temporary or permanent residence, depending on its wording.

Index

About the Author

William Macomber has served in high diplomatic office under the last five presidents—Eisenhower, Kennedy, Johnson, Nixon and Ford. He was born in Rochester, New York and served in the U.S. Marine Corps in World War II. At that time he decided that peacemaking would be his career. He completed his undergraduate work at Yale and holds graduate degrees from Harvard and the University of Chicago. In 1955, he became special assistant to Secretary of State John Foster Dulles, in 1957 Assistant Secretary of State (for Congressional Relations). In 1961, he was sent to Jordan, Kennedy's only Republican ambassadorial appointment at the start of his new administration. Since that time he has served continuously either as Assistant Secretary or Ambassador. He is currently United States Ambassador to Turkey.

Ambassador Macomber is married to the former Phyllis Bernau, a gifted diplomatic partner and once secretary to Secretaries Dulles and Rusk.